KANTAR FOR THE DEFENSE

VOLUME 2

Edwin B. Kantar

Published by
Melvin Powers
WILSHIRE BOOK COMPANY
12015 Sherman Road
No. Hollywood, California 91605
Telephone: (213) 875-1711 / (818) 983-1105

Printed by
HAL LEIGHTON PRINTING COMPANY
P.O. Box 3952
North Hollywood, California 91605
Telephone: (213) 983-1105

Printed in the United States of America
Library of Congress Catalog Card Number: 82-63189
ISBN 0-87980-409-2

FOREWORD

For those of you who worked your way through "Kantar for the Defense," Volume I, this book should seem like an old shoe, comfortable.

The problems are considerably more difficult, but certainly not beyond your towering defensive capabilities. Some new themes have been introduced, but the format is the same as in Volume I.

To review, your opponents are playing a standard system unless otherwise mentioned. In particular, they are using a 15–17 point one notrump opening bid range, a 20 to a bad 22 two notrump opening bid range, 7–10 point weak two bids, and a forcing opening bid of 2♣. (Sorry, Precision and other strong One Club players.) First and second seat major suit opening bids will generally be made with five card suits (or longer) although if the hand screams for a four card major suit opening, so be it.

As for you and your partner, you still have not been able to convince him to play upside down attitude signals. Oh, well. One day!

You are leading fourth best, the lead of a jack denies a higher honor, and the lead of a nine or a ten shows either top or two higher honors. In the case of the ten, the lead will be either top of a sequence or from KJ10 or AJ10 combinations. The lead of the nine will be either top of a sequence or from Q109, K109, or A109 combinations. You are also leading the king from ace-king, this one with reservations. As in Vol. I, from AKQ combinations, the queen will be led.

As in most defensive problems, the premium is on counting, counting tricks, points and distributions. Positive and negative inferences abound. Also, knowing basic card combinations as well as being aware of entry problems certainly won't hurt.

For your own benefit, answer each question before going on to the next. Frequently the answer to the previous question will be found in the following question.

In the rare instance where you actually make a defensive error, consult the list of themes for each of the 100 problems listed in the back of the book. If certain errors reoccur, you can isolate the theme and know what you have to work on.

Four final tips:

(1) Assume the contract can be defeated.

(2) Don't be greedy. Take the safe play to defeat the contract, not the risky one.

(3) Do not worry about letting them make overtricks.

(4) Don't tackle these problems if you are tired, even a little!

Edwin B. Kantar
Los Angeles

CONTENTS

PAGE

PAGE

PAGE

(1) LEADING THEIR SUIT

Both sides vulnerable
Dealer South

North
♠ A 10 9 8
♡ Q 5
♢ A K 7
♣ A K 10 8

East (you)
♠ K J
♡ 10 6 3
♢ Q J 9 4
♣ Q 7 6 3

South	**West**	**North**	**East**
Pass	Pass	1♣	Pass
1♠	Pass	4♠	All Pass

Opening lead: ♣5

Declarer wins in dummy, playing the ♣4 from his hand. Dummy plays the ace and a spade to your king, partner following with the ♠4 and the ♠3.

1. Where are the heart honors?
2. Can you see any way of getting four tricks?
3. What do you return at trick four?

LEADING THEIR SUIT (Solution)

North
♠ A 10 9 8
♡ Q 5
◊ A K 7
♣ A K 10 8

West
♠ 5 4 3
♡ A J 7 4 2
◊ 8 5 3 2
♣ 5

East
♠ K J
♡ 10 6 3
◊ Q J 9 4
♣ Q 7 6 3

South
♠ Q 7 6 2
♡ K 9 8
◊ 10 6
♣ J 9 4 2

1. Either South has both heart honors or they are split. If partner had them (1) he would have led the suit; (2) South would not have had enough high card points to scrape up a vulnerable one spade response.

2–3. There is a chance for four defensive tricks if partner started with a singleton club. Return your *lowest* club, making sure partner returns a diamond after ruffing. If partner ruffs, you defeat the hand if partner started with 3–5–4–1 distribution as well as the ♡AJ, or if he started with 3–6–3–1 distribution with either the ♡A or the ♡K.

KEY LESSON POINTERS

1. THE HIGH-LOW IN THE TRUMP SUIT SHOWS AN ODD NUMBER OF TRUMPS WHEN GIVING COUNT IS THE ISSUE. WHEN LOOKING FOR A RUFF, THE HIGH-LOW ANNOUNCES POSSESSION OF AT LEAST A THIRD TRUMP. HOWEVER, (EXCEPTION COMING UP) WHEN AN OBVIOUS SHORT SUIT IS LED THE PLAYER LOOKING FOR THE RUFF SHOULD NOT HIGH-LOW WHEN HOLDING A DOUBLETON AND THE OPPONENTS HAVE THE HIGHEST REMAINING CARD IN THE SUIT. THE HIGH-LOW IN THAT CASE IS RESERVED FOR A SINGLETON. FOR EXAMPLE, IF WEST HAD LED FROM A DOUBLETON CLUB WITH THE HIGH CLUB VISIBLE, HE SHOULD NOT HIGH-LOW IN TRUMPS.
2. AFTER YOU DECIDE TO GIVE YOUR PARTNER A RUFF, DO NOT GET CARELESS. YOUR RETURN IS A SUIT PREFERENCE PLAY.

(2) LISTENING

East-West vulnerable
Dealer South

North
♠ 4 2
♡ A J 5
◇ K Q J 10 9
♣ 7 4 2

West (you)
♠ 6 5
♡ K 8 3
◇ 8 6 4 3
♣ A K J 10

South	West	North	East
2 ♣	Pass	3 ◇	Pass
3 ♠	Pass	4 ♡	Pass
4 NT	Pass	5 ◇	Pass
6 ♠	All Pass		

Opening lead: ♣ K

Partner plays the ♣ 3 and declarer the ♣ Q.

1. What do you play now? Why?

LISTENING (Solution)

North
♠ 4 2
♡ A J 5
◊ K Q J 10 9
♣ 7 4 2

West
♠ 6 5
♡ K 8 3
◊ 8 6 4 3
♣ A K J 10

East
♠ 3
♡ Q 9 4 2
◊ 7 5 2
♣ 9 8 6 5 3

South
♠ A K Q J 10 9 8 7
♡ 10 7 6
◊ A
♣ Q

1. The ♡K, or almost as good, a low heart.

   Declarer cannot have two losing clubs for his bidding and the only realistic chance is to knock out dummy's heart entry in case the diamonds are blocked. Why the ♡K?

   In order for any heart play to be right, partner needs the ♡Q. If you lead low and dummy plays low, partner with Q9x(x) might err and play the ♡9. Why take any chances?

KEY LESSON POINTERS

1. ASSUME A SANE DECLARER WILL NOT LEAP TO SLAM WITH TWO QUICK LOSERS IN AN UNBID SUIT.
2. ASSUME AN ALERT PARTNER WILL MAKE A LEAD-DIRECTING DOUBLE OF A SLAM CONTRACT WITH A VOID IN DUMMY'S FIRST BID SUIT. NO DOUBLE-NO VOID.
3. WHEN THINGS LOOK HOPELESS, TRY TO IMAGINE SOMETHING GOOD. HERE YOU MUST IMAGINE THAT THE DIAMONDS ARE BLOCKED AND TRY TO DO SOMETHING ABOUT IT.
4. IF POSSIBLE, DO NOT GIVE PARTNER A CHANCE TO MAKE AN ERROR NO MATTER HOW FAR-FETCHED. PARTNERS HAVE A WAY . . .

(3) DIFFERENT STROKES FOR DIFFERENT FOLKS

North-South vulnerable
Dealer North

North
♠ A J 10 3
♡ 7 6
♢ J 10 8
♣ A Q 10 9

East (you)
♠ K 9 8
♡ A Q 9 4 3
♢ 3 2
♣ 7 6 5

North	East	South	West
1 ♣	1 ♡	2 NT*	Pass
3 NT	All Pass		

*13–15

Opening lead: ♡2

Plan your defense.

DIFFERENT STROKES FOR DIFFERENT FOLKS (Solution)

North
♠ A J 10 3
♡ 7 6
♢ J 10 8
♣ A Q 10 9

West
♠ 7 6 5
♡ J 8 2
♢ K 7 6 5
♣ 4 3 2

East
♠ K 9 8
♡ A Q 9 4 3
♢ 3 2
♣ 7 6 5

South
♠ Q 4 2
♡ K 10 5
♢ A Q 9 4
♣ K J 8

Two defenses are possible: (1) Win the ♡A and shift to a diamond playing partner for ♢AQxxx. Assuming partner ducks this trick, when in with the ♠K you will be able to return your second diamond and defeat the contract. You are playing declarer for: ♠Qxx ♡KJx ♢Kxx ♣KJxx. (2) Play the ♡Q at trick one (to prevent declarer from holding up with ♡K10x) and continue with a low heart if the queen holds. If the queen loses and you get in with the ♠K, lead a low heart playing partner for ♡Jxx. Of course, if declarer started with ♡KJ doubleton you will be explaining this play away for years to come. If partner gets in first, his second heart play will clarify the position.

Which play is better? The one that works! Kidding. Play (2) is better because it requires much less in partner's hand. Also, partner might have led a diamond holding ♢AQxxx and ♡xxx. Not likely, but possible.

KEY LESSON POINTERS

1. WHEN YOU MUST CHOOSE BETWEEN TWO LINES OF DEFENSE, SELECT THE ONE THAT REQUIRES THE LEAST FROM PARTNER. (HE NEVER HAS WHAT YOU WANT HIM TO HAVE ANYWAY.)
2. WHEN HOLDING AQxxx IN THE SUIT PARTNER HAS LED AND YOU WISH TO ESTABLISH, PLAY THE QUEEN IN ORDER TO PREVENT DECLARER FROM HOLDING UP WITH K10x.
3. MAKE SURE YOU KNOW WHICH CARD YOUR PARTNER WILL LEAD FROM THREE SMALL IN YOUR SUIT VS. NOTRUMP.

(4) SEQUENCES

North-South vulnerable
Dealer South

North
♠ 9 8 6 5
♡ 7 4
◊ A K J 5 2
♣ J 2

East (you)
♠ Q J 10 7
♡ A 9 3 2
◊ Q 7 3
♣ 9 5

South	**West**	**North**	**East**
1 ♣	Pass	1 ◊	Pass
3 NT*	All Pass		

*Solid minor

Opening lead: ♡Q

1. Which heart do you play at trick one? Why?
2. You win the ♡A, declarer following with the ♡6. What do you return at trick two? Why?

SEQUENCES (Solution)

North
♠ 9 8 6 5
♡ 7 4
◊ A K J 5 2
♣ J 2

West
♠ A 3 2
♡ Q J 10 8 5
◊ 9 8 6
♣ 7 4

East
♠ Q J 10 7
♡ A 9 3 2
◊ Q 7 3
♣ 9 5

South
♠ K 4
♡ K 6
◊ 10 4
♣ A K Q 10 8 6 3

1. The ♡A for two reasons: (1) Declarer may have a singleton king, or (2) if he does not, a shift is necessary, as at least nine tricks are staring you in the face—six or seven clubs, two diamonds and a heart.
2. The ♠7. You need *four* spade tricks to defeat the contract so you must play partner for Axx or Axxx. By leading low you give yourself a chance for four tricks. If you lead the ♠Q you have no chance as dummy's nine stands up as a fourth round stopper.

KEY LESSON POINTERS

1. AFTER A MINOR SUIT OPENING, AND A ONE LEVEL RESPONSE, A JUMP TO THREE NOTRUMP IS BASED ON A LONG SOLID MINOR AND IS NOT A HUGE POINT COUNT BID.
2. ONCE THE DUMMY IS IN VIEW, IT MAY BE NECESSARY TO ATTACK A SUIT WITH A SEEMINGLY ABNORMAL CARD TO REALIZE THE DESIRED NUMBER OF TRICKS.
3. IF YOU PLAY THE LEAD CONVENTION THAT THE QUEEN VS. NOTRUMP ASKS PARTNER TO UNBLOCK THE JACK, DO NOT USE THE CONVENTION VS. GAMBLING-TYPE NOTRUMP BIDDING. FOR EXAMPLE, HOW WOULD YOU EXPLAIN YOUR BRILLIANT DEFENSE ON THIS HAND IF PARTNER TURNED UP WITH ♡KQ10xx?

(5) HE KNOWS WHAT HE KNOWS

East-West vulnerable
Dealer West

North
♠ K J 8 4
♡ A 10 7 5 3
♢ Q 8 2
♣ 6

West (you)
♠ Q 2
♡ J 4
♢ A K 9 5 3
♣ J 8 7 4

West	**North**	**East**	**South**
Pass	Pass	Pass	1 ♡
Pass	4 ♡	All Pass	

Opening lead: ♢ K

1. Partner plays the ♢4 and declarer the ♢6. What do you play at trick two?

HE KNOWS WHAT HE KNOWS (Solution)

North
♠ K J 8 4
♡ A 10 7 5 3
♢ Q 8 2
♣ 6

West
♠ Q 2
♡ J 4
♢ A K 9 5 3
♣ J 8 7 4

East
♠ A 10 5 3
♡ 6
♢ J 10 4
♣ K 10 5 3 2

South
♠ 9 7 6
♡ K Q 9 8 2
♢ 7 6
♣ A Q 9

There are a couple of possibilities: (1) Partner has a singleton diamond and a black ace. In that case cashing the ♢A is the winning play. (2) Partner has three diamonds and ♠A10xx. In that case a shift to the ♠Q is necessary before declarer builds up a diamond discard by leading up to the ♢Q. This defense seems a bit more logical.

If you do switch to the ♠Q at trick two, partner must retain communication with your hand by ducking when dummy plays the king.

How will he know that your ♠Q is not a singleton? A player of your demonstrated skills would have cashed the ♢A before leading a singleton spade. Once you fail to do this, partner will know you have a doubleton.

KEY LESSON POINTERS

1. DECLARER KNOWS A CERTAIN AMOUNT ABOUT YOUR HONOR STRENGTH FROM THE BIDDING. FOR EXAMPLE, ONCE YOU PASSED ORIGINALLY AND THEN LED THE ♢K, DECLARER WILL ASSUME PARTNER HAS THE ♠A. THEREFORE, IT WOULD BE FUTILE TO LEAD THE ♠2 HOPING TO DECEIVE DECLARER.
2. DEFENDERS FREQUENTLY MUST RETAIN COMMUNICATION WITH PARTNER'S HAND BY DUCKING A WINNER WHEN THEY HAVE NO OUTSIDE ENTRY TO THE SUIT THEY WISH TO SCORE TRICKS IN. (EAST MUST DUCK THE ♠K IN ORDER TO REALIZE TWO SPADE TRICKS.)
3. IN GENERAL, WHEN YOU FEAR THAT DECLARER IS GOING TO DISCARD A LOSER ON AN ESTABLISHED, OR AN EVENTUALLY ESTABLISHED WINNER IN DUMMY, SHIFT TO DUMMY'S LONGER SIDE SUIT, IN THIS CASE, SPADES RATHER THAN CLUBS. DECLARER CAN'T HURT YOU BY DISCARDING A CLUB FROM HIS HAND ON THE ♢Q, BUT A SPADE DISCARD COULD BE FATAL.

(6) 2 FOR THE PRICE OF 1

North-South vulnerable
Dealer East

North
♠ K 9 6
♡ K 6
◊ 8 2
♣ A K J 10 7 2

West (you)
♠ Q 8 4
♡ A Q 9 7 3
◊ Q J 10
♣ 4 3

East	**South**	**West**	**North**
Pass	Pass	1 ♡	2 ♣
Pass	2 NT	Pass	3 NT
All Pass			

Opening lead: ◊Q

Partner plays the ◊3 and declarer wins the ◊K. At trick two declarer leads a low heart.

1. Which heart do you play? Why?
2. Assume you win the ♡A and partner plays the ♡4. What do you play now?
3. Visualize a dummy that started with one less club, and one more small heart. Again you lead the ◊Q, but this time partner plays the ◊7. Declarer wins with the ◊K and plays a low heart. Now, how do you defend?

2 FOR THE PRICE OF 1 (Solution)

North
♠ K 9 6
♡ K 6
◊ 8 2
♣ A K J 10 7 2

West
♠ Q 8 4
♡ A Q 9 7 3
◊ Q J 10
♣ 4 3

East
♠ A J 10 2
♡ 4 2
◊ 9 7 6 4 3
♣ 6 5

South
♠ 7 5 3
♡ J 10 8 3
◊ A K 5
♣ Q 9 8

1. The ♡A. Partner's low diamond at trick one has denied the ace so declarer has two tricks in that suit. You can infer from his failure to attack clubs that he has the queen. Ergo, South is going for his ninth trick before you have time to compose yourself.
2. The ♠Q. You are too smart to be caught napping. Your only chance is to go for four spade tricks. Partner needs the magic holding of ♠AJ10x. Rise with the ♡A and triumphantly place the ♠Q on the table. Everyone will be so impresed.
3. This time partner has the ◊A, and once again declarer is trying to steal his ninth trick. You can count declarer for two spades (if partner has the ◊A, declarer has the ♠A), five clubs and one diamond so far. Jump up and continue with the ◊J hoping partner has at least five diamonds.

KEY LESSON POINTERS

1. WHEN AN HONOR IS LED VS. NOTRUMP, THIRD HAND GIVES ATTITUDE, NOT COUNT.
2. FROM PARTNER'S TRICK ONE ATTITUDE PLAY, THE OPENING LEADER CAN FREQUENTLY COUNT THE NUMBER OF TRICKS DECLARER HAS AVAILABLE IN THE SUIT LED.
3. WHEN DECLARER LEAVES A LONG STRONG SUIT UNTOUCHED, PRESUME HE HAS ANY MISSING HONOR.
4. TRICK COUNTING IS VERY IMPORTANT, BUT NEVER MORE SO THAN WHEN A LONG STRONG SUIT HITS THE TABLE AND YOU ARE DEFENDING NOTRUMP.

(7) A VOTE OF CONFIDENCE

Both sides vulnerable
Dealer South

North
♠ 9 5
♡ 8 5
◇ A J 10 7 4
♣ A Q 4 3

East (you)
♠ J 4 3 2
♡ Q J 9
◇ K 2
♣ 10 7 5 2

South	**West**	**North**	**East**
1 NT	Pass	3 NT	All Pass

Opening lead: ♡7

You play the ♡J and declarer wins with the ♡K. At trick two declarer runs the ◇9 to your ◇K, partner playing the ◇6.

1. What card do you play to trick three? Why?

A VOTE OF CONFIDENCE (Solution)

North
♠ 9 5
♡ 8 5
◊ A J 10 7 4
♣ A Q 4 3

West
♠ A Q 10 6
♡ 10 7 6 3
◊ 6 5
♣ 9 8 6

East
♠ J 4 3 2
♡ Q J 9
◊ K 2
♣ 10 7 5 2

South
♠ K 8 7
♡ A K 4 2
◊ Q 9 8 3
♣ K J

1. The ♠J. Partner has not led a fourth best heart — the rule of 11 tells you so. If it is not fourth best it is either top of three or four small, second best from 10xxx, or low from A107. In any case there is no future in hearts. In fact, there is an excellent chance that declarer has at least nine tricks ready to go — four diamonds, three clubs along with at least two hearts. Clearly the only hope is spades and you must attack with the ♠J to retain the lead in case partner has ♠AQ10x. If you lead low, declarer will play safe by ducking the lead into partner's hand.

KEY LESSON POINTERS

1. DON'T AUTOMATICALLY ASSUME PARTNER IS LEADING FOURTH BEST. CHECK THE LEAD BY USING THE RULE OF ELEVEN. IF IT DOESN'T CHECK OUT, ALLOW FOR PARTNER TO BE LEADING SECOND HIGH FROM FOUR CARDS HEADED BY THE NINE OR TEN, OR TOP OF THREE OR FOUR SMALL.
2. WHEN ON LEAD FOR THE LAST TIME, CONSIDER LEADING YOUR HONOR FROM HOLDINGS SUCH AS 10xx, Jxx, or Qxx WHEN TWO OR THREE SMALL CARDS ARE TO YOUR RIGHT. NOW DECLARER CANNOT DUCK THE LEAD INTO PARTNER'S HAND. IN FACT, LEADING LOW IN THESE SITUATIONS GUARANTEES THE ACE OR KING.

(8) STRANGE PREFERENCE

East-West vulnerable
Dealer South

North
♠ J 9 7 6 5
♡ Q 2
◊ A Q J 4
♣ 3 2

West (you)
♠ A K Q 10 2
♡ K 3
◊ 9 8
♣ Q 9 5 4

South	**West**	**North**	**East**
1 ♡	1 ♠	1 NT	Pass
2 ◊	Pass	3 ♡!	Pass
4 ♡	All Pass		

Opening lead: ♠Q

You continue with a second high spade which declarer ruffs with the ♡8. Declarer follows with the ♣AK and a low club ruffing with dummy's ♡Q, partner playing high-low.

1. What is declarer's distribution?
   Declarer leads a trump to his jack and your king, partner playing the four.
2. What do you play now?

STRANGE PREFERENCE (Solution)

North
♠ J 9 7 6 5
♡ Q 2
◊ A Q J 4
♣ 3 2

West
♠ A K Q 10 2
♡ K 3
◊ 9 8
♣ Q 9 5 4

East
♠ 8 3
♡ 7 6 5 4
◊ 7 6 2
♣ J 10 8 5

South
♠ 4
♡ A J 10 9 8
◊ K 10 5 3
♣ A K 6

1. 1 –5 –4 –3.
2. Your remaining high spade.

At the point you win the ♡K both declarer and your partner have three trumps. By playing a high spade you allow your partner to discard a diamond. After declarer ruffs and plays his remaining trumps, partner will ruff the *third* diamond with the game's last trump and cash a club for the setting trick.

If, instead of a high spade, you play the ♣Q, declarer will ruff, draw trumps and take three diamond tricks instead of two. He also will make the hand instead of going down one. The less said about a diamond return, the better.

KEY LESSON POINTERS

1. WHEN BOTH PARTNER AND DECLARER HAVE THE SAME NUMBER OF TRUMPS AND YOU CAN FORCE THE DECLARER IN ONE OF TWO SUITS, (PARTNER HAVING ONE OF THOSE SUITS) PLAY THE SUIT PARTNER DOESN'T HAVE. IN THIS WAY PARTNER CAN DISCARD A LOSER LIMITING DECLARER TO ONE LESS TRICK IN THE SUIT PARTNER DISCARDS.

(9) THE FIRST THREE

North-South vulnerable
Dealer East

North
♠ A Q
♡ Q J 9 8 7
◇ 10 5 4
♣ Q 5 4

East (you)
♠ J 3 2
♡ 10 6 5
◇ A K 9 8
♣ 10 9 8

East	South	West	North
Pass	1 ♠	Pass	2 ♡
Pass	2 ♠	Pass	3 ♠
Pass	4 ♠	All Pass	

Opening lead: ◇Q

You signal smartly with the ◇9 and partner continues with the ◇J. You overtake and cash a third diamond, all following.

1. Now what?

THE FIRST THREE (Solution)

North
♠ A Q
♡ Q J 9 8 7
♢ 10 5 4
♣ Q 5 4

West
♠ 10 5
♡ 4 3 2
♢ Q J 2
♣ K J 7 3 2

East
♠ J 3 2
♡ 10 6 5
♢ A K 9 8
♣ 10 9 8

South
♠ K 9 8 7 6 4
♡ A K
♢ 7 6 3
♣ A 6

1. Your best shot is a fourth diamond.

This wins outright anytime partner has the ♠10 as declarer will have to ruff in dummy and your ♠J will be promoted. It also works when declarer has ♠K108xx(x) and ruffs with the ♠8, allowing partner to overtrump with the ♠9.

As declarer cannot afford to discard a loser and ruff in dummy, the only time your play loses is when partner has the ♣A and declarer the ♡AKx along with the ♠K10. (Rather unlikely as South would have supported hearts with that hand.) If you don't play a diamond declarer will make the hand by discarding his losing club on a heart.

KEY LESSON POINTERS

1. A RUFF AND SLUFF CAN BE A DEVASTATING DEFENSIVE PLAY WHEN THE RUFF MUST BE TAKEN WITH A HIGH HONOR THUS PROMOTING A TRUMP TRICK FOR THE DEFENSE.

(10) SPLITTING HONORS

Both sides vulnerable
Dealer North

North
♠ A K 9 8 4
♡ K 7 2
◊ Q 10 4
♣ J 3

West (you)
♠ Q J 10 5
♡ 6 5 3
◊ 6 5
♣ A K 10 7

North	East	South	West
1 ♠	Pass	2 ♡	Pass
3 ♡	Pass	4 ♡	All Pass

Opening lead: ♣K

You continue with a second club which declarer ruffs. Declarer exits with the ♡Q to partner's ace. Partner exits with a heart and declarer plays a third trump ending in his hand, partner discarding a club.

1. What are declarer's possible distributions?
2. Declarer leads a low spade. Do you split your honors? Why, or why not?

SPLITTING HONORS (Solution)

North
♠ A K 9 8 4
♡ K 7 2
♢ Q 10 4
♣ J 3

West
♠ Q J 10 5
♡ 6 5 3
♢ 6 5
♣ A K 10 7

East
♠ 7
♡ A 8
♢ J 9 8 2
♣ Q 9 8 6 5 4

South
♠ 6 3 2
♡ Q J 10 9 4
♢ A K 7 3
♣ 2

1. Declarer must be 2–5–5–1 or 3–5–4–1.
2. No. If declarer has the first distribution he is not about to finesse the ♠9. He is simply entering dummy to make a diamond play. In fact, it doesn't matter whether you split or not against this distribution.

   However, if declarer has the other distribution, the critical one, you must not split. If you do, declarer will win and exit with the ♠9. Now your remaining spade honor is finesseable and any losing diamond can be discarded on the spades. (Declarer should have the ♢AK.) If, on the other hand, you play low, declarer's proper percentage play with this combination is to win the ace hoping East has a singleton honor (or the suit splits 3–2). Once declarer plays the ace from dummy his goose is cooked. He can duck a spade to you, but all you need do is play a club forcing out declarer's last trump. Now a diamond trick must be lost.

KEY LESSON POINTERS

1. IF YOU KNOW DECLARER'S DISTRIBUTION, YOU OFTEN KNOW HOW HE IS GOING TO TACKLE A PARTICULAR SUIT.
2. KEEP TRACK OF THE NUMBER OF TRUMPS DECLARER HAS AT ANY GIVEN MOMENT. IMPORTANTISIMO.

(11) INFERENCES

Both sides vulnerable
Dealer West

North
♠ 10 8 3 2
♡ A 6 5
◇ K 5
♣ J 10 8 7

East (you)
♠ 4
♡ Q 8 7 3 2
◇ A 6 3 2
♣ 9 6 2

West	North	East	South
Pass	Pass	Pass	1 ♣
Dbl.	1 NT	2 ♡	2 ♠
3 ♡	3 ♠	4 ♡	4 ♠
All Pass			

Opening lead: ♡10 (Zero or two higher honors)

1. Dummy wins the ♡A, declarer following with the ♡4. Which heart do you play?

   At trick two a spade is led to the queen which holds, and at trick three declarer leads the ♠J to partner's ♠K, as you discard the ◇6.
2. Partner shifts to the ◇Q which is covered and taken by your ace, declarer playing the ◇7. What do you play now?

INFERENCES (Solution)

North
♠ 10 8 3 2
♡ A 6 5
◇ K 5
♣ J 10 8 7

West
♠ K 9 6 5
♡ K J 10 9
◇ Q J 9 8 4
♣ —

East
♠ 4
♡ Q 8 7 3 2
◇ A 6 3 2
♣ 9 6 2

South
♠ A Q J 7
♡ 4
◇ 10 7
♣ A K Q 5 4 3

1. The ♡2. Give count when partner knows your honor holding. Partner knows you have the ♡Q when the ace is played from dummy.
2. The ♣9. Partner is marked with one of two hand patterns: 4–4–4–1 or 4–4–5–0. If he has the first, the hand cannot be beaten. If he has the second, you can give him a club ruff. His ◇J will then be the setting trick.

   The reason you returned the ♣9, your highest club, was that you did not want partner to underlead his ◇J over to your nonexistent ◇10 looking for another ruff. Trusting partners have an irritating habit of doing things like that.

   Notice, without your count signal at trick one, partner might try to cash the ♡K rather than the ◇J for the setting trick. In fact, he should!

KEY LESSON POINTERS

1. WHEN DECLARER'S PLAY FROM DUMMY MARKS YOU, THIRD HAND, WITH A PARTICULAR HONOR, GIVE COUNT. IF IT DOESN'T, GIVE ATTITUDE.
2. BE VERY CAREFUL WHEN GIVING A GOOD PARTNER A RUFF. THE CARD YOU PLAY IS A SUIT PREFERENCE SIGNAL. HE MAY BELIEVE YOU.
3. DON'T GLOAT OVER GOOD DEFENSES. FOR EXAMPLE, ONE OF YOUR OPPONENTS MIGHT REMIND YOU—GENTLY—THAT YOUR SIDE IS ON FOR 5♡!

(12) THE WEAK TWO IN ACTION

Both sides vulnerable
Dealer West

North
♠ 10 5
♡ A K 8
◊ 9 6 5 3
♣ 8 6 5 4

East (you)
♠ 6 2
♡ J 10 9 7 5
◊ A Q 8 4
♣ 9 3

West	North	East	South
2 ♠	Pass	Pass	2 NT*
Pass	3 NT	All Pass	

*15–18

Opening lead: ♠Q

1. Which spade do you play?
2. Declarer wins the ♠K, who has the ♠A?
3. Declarer leads the ♡4 to the ♡K, which heart do you play? A low club is led from dummy and declarer's ♣Q loses to the ♣K. Partner exits with the ◊10, dummy playing low.
4. Which diamond do you play? What is your plan?

THE WEAK TWO IN ACTION (Solution)

North
♠ 10 5
♡ A K 8
◊ 9 6 5 3
♣ 8 6 5 4

West
♠ Q J 9 7 4 3
♡ 6 3
◊ K 10 2
♣ K 2

East
♠ 6 2
♡ J 10 9 7 5
◊ A Q 8 4
♣ 9 3

South
♠ A K 8
♡ Q 4 2
◊ J 7
♣ A Q J 10 7

1. The ♠2. Attitude when partner leads an honor vs. notrump and dummy has small cards. (If dummy had ♠A K blank, for example, you would signal count because you couldn't have an honor.)
2. You can't tell. Partner could be leading from a QJ9 or an AQJ combination. Notice how third hand remains temporarily in the dark when declarer wins the king as opposed to the ace.
3. The ♡J. To show your sequence as well as to allow partner to count tricks.
4. The ◊A— unless declarer is a close relative. This is what you know: (1) Partner must have led spades from a QJ combination or else he would have cashed his spade winners; (2) declarer is marked with the ♡Q, from partner's failure to lead that suit after your honor signal; (3) if partner had a second club trick, he would have continued spades to set up his suit.

   Since there is such a good chance that declarer has nine tricks outside of diamonds, you must play for four diamond tricks and assume partner has started an unblock from K10x. Win the ace and return a low diamond.

KEY LESSON POINTERS

1. WHEN PARTNER LEADS AN HONOR CARD VS. NOTRUMP, AND DUMMY HAS SMALL CARDS, SIGNAL ATTITUDE.
2. WHEN DECLARER (OR DUMMY) WINS A TRICK AND PARTNER FOLLOWS WITH AN UNNECESSARILY HIGH HONOR, ASSUME HE HAS THE MISSING LOWER HONORS, BUT NONE OF THE MISSING HIGHER HONORS.
3. ALLOW FOR PARTNER TO ATTACK A SUIT WITH A MIDDLE CARD FROM HOLDINGS THAT INCLUDE ONE HIGH HONOR, ONE HIGH MIDDLE SPOT CARD, AND ONE LOW CARD. IT MIGHT BE A NECESSARY UNBLOCK PLAY FOR YOUR LONGER PRESUMED HOLDING.

(13) AND NOW?

East-West vulnerable
Dealer South

North
♠ Q 8
♡ 9 8 7
♢ K Q 9 2
♣ K J 8 7

West (you)
♠ K J 7 6 3
♡ Q 2
♢ 10 4 3
♣ 9 6 4

South	West	North	East
1 ♡	Pass	2 ♣	Pass
3 ♣	Pass	3 ♡	Pass
4 ♢	Pass	4 ♡	All Pass

Opening lead: ♠6

Partner wins the ♠A and returns the ♠2 to your king.

1. What are declarer's most likely distributions?
2. What do you play to trick three?

AND NOW? (Solution)

North
♠ Q 8
♡ 9 8 7
◇ K Q 9 2
♣ K J 8 7

West
♠ K J 7 6 3
♡ Q 2
◇ 10 4 3
♣ 9 6 4

East
♠ A 9 4 2
♡ J 4 3
◇ J 7 6 5
♣ Q 5

South
♠ 10 5
♡ A K 10 6 5
◇ A 8
♣ A 10 3 2

1. Declarer's possible distributions are: (a) 2–5–3–3, (b) 2–6–1–4, (c) 2–6–2–3, (d) plus the most likely of all, 2–5–2–4.
2. The idea is to exit safely. The only "safe" suit is diamonds. If declarer has the singleton ace or Axx it doesn't matter which diamond you lead. However, if declarer has specifically ◇A8 (guess what?), you must exit with the ◇10 so that you won't present declarer with four diamond tricks and thus obviate a possible club guess.

   Double dummy, declarer can actually overcome this play by winning the ◇A, cashing the ♡A and then playing two more diamonds, discarding a club. A heart is now ducked to your queen and you've had it. However, if declarer actually plays that way, you should either: (1) hold your cards back; (2) play in an easier game.

KEY LESSON POINTERS

1. ALWAYS TRY TO WORK OUT DECLARER'S DISTRIBUTION FROM THE BIDDING. AFTER THE FIRST FEW TRICKS, PARTNER'S CARDS GIVE YOU ADDITIONAL INFORMATION. FOR EXAMPLE, PARTNER SHOWED TWO OR FOUR SPADES BY RETURNING THE DEUCE.
2. WHEN LEADING THROUGH A STRONGISH FOUR CARD HOLDING IN DUMMY IT IS FREQUENTLY RIGHT TO ATTACK WITH AN HONOR WHEN HOLDING 10xx, Jxx, or Qxx. THESE LEADS WORK PARTICULARLY WELL WHEN PARTNER HAS FOUR CARDS IN THE SUIT.

(14) ALL THE CARDS

North-South vulnerable
Dealer North

North
♠ Q 10 9
♡ Q J
◇ 7 6 4 3 2
♣ 10 9 8

West (you)
♠ K J 8 6 3
♡ A K
◇ A 9 8
♣ Q 4 3

North	East	South	West
Pass	Pass	1 NT	Dbl.
All Pass			

Opening lead: ♠6

Dummy plays the ♠9, partner the ♠7 and declarer the ♠5.

1. What do you make of the spade position?

   A low diamond is led to the king and ace, partner playing the jack. You cash your top hearts partner playing the ♡2 and the ♡9.

2. Who has the ◇Q?
3. How do you read the heart position?

   You exit with a diamond to declarer's queen, partner furnishing the ◇10. At trick six declarer exits with a diamond which you win, partner discarding the ♣6.

4. What do you play to trick seven?

ALL THE CARDS (Solution)

North
♠ Q 10 9
♡ Q J
♢ 7 6 4 3 2
♣ 10 9 8

West
♠ K J 8 6 3
♡ A K
♢ A 9 8
♣ Q 4 3

East
♠ 7 2
♡ 9 8 7 3 2
♢ J 10
♣ J 6 5 2

South
♠ A 5 4
♡ 10 6 5 4
♢ K Q 5
♣ A K 7

1. Partner has either a singleton or a doubleton spade.
2. Declarer. With equal honors defenders should split with the higher, not the lower, equal.
3. Partner has five hearts headed by the 987. The ♡2 was attitude, the ♡9, present count. Partner could not have afforded the ♡9 unless he had a sequence.
4. The ♣Q! Now that you have put all this information together, you must make a play that will keep you off lead forever. In order to defeat the contract, partner needs but one card, the ♣J. Wiggle as he might after the lead of the ♣Q, declarer can no longer prevent your partner from getting the lead in either clubs or hearts to make a killing spade play. Had you led a low club, then you, not partner, would have been thrown in with a club and forced to lead a spade or vice versa. Yes, had you continued spades at every opportunity you also would have defeated the contract one trick. But this way you had a chance to make a brilliancy!

KEY LESSON POINTERS

1. THIRD HAND GIVES COUNT WHEN PARTNER LEADS LOW AND DUMMY WINS THE TRICK WITH THE QUEEN OR LESS; ATTITUDE IF DUMMY WINS WITH AN UNSUPPORTED ACE OR KING.
2. WHEN SPLITTING HONORS, DEFENDERS SHOULD SPLIT WITH THEIR HIGHEST, NOT THEIR LOWEST EQUAL. IF SECOND HAND HOLDS Q J 10 9 AND DUMMY LEADS LOW, THE QUEEN IS THE MOST INFORMATIVE CARD TO PLAY. WHAT WILL PARTNER KNOW IF YOU PLAY THE NINE?
3. WHEN YOU LEAD A HIGH HONOR (HEART ACE OR KING) PARTNER'S FIRST OBLIGATION IS ATTITUDE. HIS SECOND CARD IS PRESENT COUNT. WITH FOUR REMAINING CARDS HE PLAYS THE HIGHEST HE CAN AFFORD, WITH THREE, THE LOWEST CARD HE HAS.

(15) SHUTOUT BID

Both sides vulnerable
Dealer South

North
♠ —
♡ 8 6 2
◊ A K J 4 3
♣ Q J 9 7 6

East (you)
♠ K Q
♡ A J 7 5 4 3
◊ 9 8
♣ K 3 2

South	West	North	East
4 ♠	All Pass		

Opening lead: ♡Q

You win the ♡A and declarer plays the ♡9.

1. What do you play at trick two? Why?
2. You return the ♣K, declarer plays the ♣4 and partner the ♣5. Now what?

SHUTOUT BID (Solution)

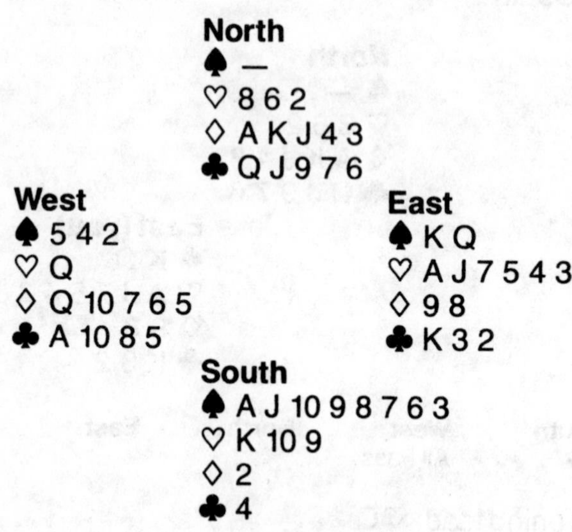

1. The ♣K. Given your spade holding, declarer figures to have an eight card suit for his vulnerable preempt. If that is the case partner must have the ♣A. Even so, you must determine whether to cash two clubs or give partner a heart ruff.

   Playing the ♣K keeps all options open. If partner has a singleton heart he will signal you with his lowest club and you will switch back to hearts. If partner has a doubleton heart he will encourage in clubs and you will return that suit.
2. When partner plays his lowest club your heart return defeats the contract one trick. True, an immediate heart return with a low club back from partner defeats the contract two tricks, and that is how to defend a contract of *three* spades. Vs. four spades no need to take such desperate measures.

KEY LESSON POINTERS

1. WHEN YOU CAN'T BE CERTAIN WHETHER OR NOT PARTNER HAS LED A SINGLETON, YOU MIGHT, IF YOU HAVE THE LUXURY, BANG DOWN A SURE WINNER IN ANOTHER SUIT. IF PARTNER PLAYS LOW IT MEANS HE HAS LED A SINGLETON AND WANTS HIS LEAD RETURNED. IF PARTNER ENCOURAGES, KISS THE SINGLETON POSSIBILITY GOODBYE.
2. THE NUMBER OF TRICKS YOU NEED TO DEFEAT A CONTRACT DETERMINES YOUR DEFENSE. THE MORE TRICKS YOU NEED, THE MORE YOU MUST FIND IN PARTNER'S HAND.
3. NOTICE PARTNER SIGNALS ATTITUDE, NOT COUNT, ON THE ♣K. IF THIS WERE A CASHOUT SITUATION (NO RUFFS INVOLVED) HE WOULD SIGNAL COUNT. IN THIS SITUATION PARTNER MUST TELL YOU WHETHER OR NOT HE HAS LED A SINGLETON—WITHOUT STARING AT YOU.

(16) VULNERABLE SLAM ON THE LINE

North-South vulnerable
Dealer South

North
♠ A K Q J 8 7
♡ 2
◇ Q 4 3
♣ J 7 5

East (you)
♠ 9 6 5
♡ 7 6 5
◇ 8 2
♣ A Q 8 4 3

South	West	North	East
1 ♡	Pass	1 ♠	Pass
3 ◇	Pass	4 ♠	Pass
4 NT	Pass	5 ◇	Pass
6 ♡	All Pass		

Opening lead: ♣2

Dummy plays low and you win the ♣A, declarer playing the ♣9.

1. What do you play to trick two, and why?

VULNERABLE SLAM ON THE LINE (Solution)

North
♠ A K Q J 8 7
♡ 2
♢ Q 4 3
♣ J 7 5

West
♠ 10 4 3
♡ 8 4 3
♢ K 7 6
♣ K 10 6 2

East
♠ 9 6 5
♡ 7 6 5
♢ 8 2
♣ A Q 8 4 3

South
♠ 2
♡ A K Q J 10 9
♢ A J 10 9 5
♣ 9

1. A spade. Dummy has shown solid spades and declarer must have solid hearts along with the ♢A and a second round club control. If you lead anything other than a spade, declarer will win, draw trumps and run the spades. However, if you lead a spade and declarer has a singleton, he will be unable to enjoy all of his spades because trumps have not been removed. The best declarer can do with a spade return is to try the diamond finesse. Down one.

KEY LESSON POINTERS

1. WHEN DUMMY COMES DOWN WITH A SOLID SUIT AND NO CERTAIN OUTSIDE ENTRY, BEST DEFENSE MAY BE TO LEAD THE SUIT EARLY TRYING TO KILL THE DISCARDS BEFORE DECLARER IS ABLE TO DRAW TRUMPS.
2. ASSUME WHEN A GOOD BIDDER BIDS A SLAM OFF AN ACE HE HAS SECOND ROUND CONTROL OF THE SUIT IN WHICH HE IS MISSING THE ACE, PLUS JOINT FIRST ROUND CONTROL OF ALL OTHER SUITS.
3. NOTICE THAT WHEN EACH HAND HAS A SOLID SUIT, IT IS BETTER TO ALLOW THE PLAYER WITH NO OUTSIDE ENTRY TO HIS SUIT (IN THIS CASE, NORTH), TO BE THE DECLARER. SIX SPADES IS EASY TO MAKE, SIX HEARTS IMPOSSIBLE AGAINST BEST DEFENSE.

(17) WEAKISH LIMIT RAISE

Neither side vulnerable
Dealer West

North
♠ 9 6 5
♡ Q 9 4 3
◇ Q 7
♣ A 8 7 5

East (you)
♠ 8 2
♡ J 5 2
◇ A J 9 8 6 3
♣ 3 2

West	North	East	South
1 ◇	Pass	3 ◇	3 ♠
All Pass			

Opening lead: ◇ 2

1. Dummy plays low, which diamond do you play? Why?
2. How do you place the heart honors around the table?
3. After winning the ◇ A, what do you play?

WEAKISH LIMIT RAISE (Solution)

North
♠ 9 6 5
♡ Q 9 4 3
◊ Q 7
♣ A 8 7 5

West
♠ A Q 7
♡ 10 8 6
◊ K 10 4 2
♣ K J 6

East
♠ 8 2
♡ J 5 2
◊ A J 9 8 6 3
♣ 3 2

South
♠ K J 10 4 3
♡ A K 7
◊ 5
♣ Q 10 9 4

1. The ◊A. Declarer just may have a singleton king.
2. Either declarer has both honors, or they are split. If partner had them both, he probably would have led the suit.
3. The ♣3. You need four more tricks to defeat this contract. Your best chance is to go for a club ruff. If partner has the ♣KJx(x) along with the ♠A and a heart trick, or two trumps tricks, including the ace, and no heart trick, you will get four more tricks.

KEY LESSON POINTERS

1. WHEN THIRD HAND CANNOT SEE THE ACE OR KING OF AN UNBID SUIT, ASSUME PARTNER DOES NOT HAVE BOTH OF THOSE CARDS. THIS REASONING ALSO APPLIES WHEN THIRD HAND CANNOT SEE THE KING OR QUEEN OF AN UNBID SUIT.
2. BEFORE MAKING ANY PLAY, ASK YOURSELF HOW MANY TRICKS YOU NEED TO DEFEAT THE CONTRACT AND WHAT YOU NEED AT THE VERY LEAST FROM PARTNER. IF IT CAN'T BE DONE IN HIGH CARDS, LOOK TO EITHER GIVE OR GET A RUFF.

(18) HE'S ALLOWED

East-West vulnerable
Dealer North

North
♠ A K Q J 10 9
♡ 7 6
◇ Q 10 8
♣ A 2

East (you)
♠ 7 6 5
♡ K 4 3
◇ A J 9
♣ K 8 7 4

North	**East**	**South**	**West**
1 ♠	Pass	1 NT	Pass
2 NT	All Pass		

Opening lead: ♣3

Dummy plays low and you win with the king, declarer playing the ♣5.

1. What do you play at trick two? Why?
2. You return the ♣4, declarer plays the ♣10 and partner the ♣J. How do you read the club suit?
3. At trick three declarer leads a low diamond from dummy. Which diamond do you play? Why?
4. You win the ◇A, partner plays the ◇2. What do you play now? Why?

HE'S ALLOWED (Solution)

North
♠ A K Q J 10 9
♡ 7 6
◊ Q 10 8
♣ A 2

West
♠ 8 3
♡ A J 9 2
◊ 6 5 2
♣ J 9 6 3

East
♠ 7 6 5
♡ K 4 3
◊ A J 9
♣ K 8 7 4

South
♠ 4 2
♡ Q 10 8 4
◊ K 7 4 3
♣ Q 10 5

1. It must be safe to return a club. If declarer has the ♡A you cannot defeat the hand, and if declarer has the ♣Q he cannot use it without first giving up the lead. You're covered.
2. Declarer has the ♣Q. If partner had the ♣QJ he would have played low (or the ♣Q if he could have afforded it). Playing a high honor unnecessarily denies a higher remaining honor. Therefore, the play of the ♣J denies the ♣Q.
3. The ◊A. Declarer is leading up to his ◊K for his eighth trick.
4. The ♡3. There is no future in either minor so you must go for four heart tricks. Your low heart play promises either the ace or king. With a lower honor you would have led the honor to prevent declarer from ducking the lead into partner's hand. Even though partner did lead from a weak club suit instead of a stronger heart suit you have come to the rescue ...again. You take four heart tricks to defeat the contract one trick.

KEY LESSON POINTERS

1. WHEN A DEFENDER PLAYS A HIGH HONOR UNNECESSARILY HE IS EITHER UNBLOCKING OR DENYING A HIGHER HONOR.
2. A DEFENDER HOLDING 10xx, Jxx, or Qxx, NEEDING THREE OR FOUR QUICK TRICKS FROM THE SUIT SHOULD LEAD THE HONOR WHEN DUMMY TO THE RIGHT HAS SMALL CARDS; LEADING LOW GUARANTEES THE ACE OR KING.

(19) TO GIVE OR TO RECEIVE?

East-West vulnerable
Dealer West

North
♠ K 3
♡ Q J 7 6
♢ A Q J 10 9
♣ 10 8

West (you)
♠ Q 10 8 5 2
♡ K 10 2
♢ 2
♣ A K Q 9

West	North	East	South
1 ♠	Dbl.	Pass	Pass*
2 ♣	Pass	3 ♣	4 ♡
All Pass			

*After some thought

Opening lead: ♣Q (You lead the Q from AKQ and partner must give count.)

1. Partner plays the ♣2. What do you think declarer's distribution is?
2. What do you play at trick two?

TO GIVE OR TO RECEIVE (Solution)

North
♠ K 3
♡ Q J 7 6
♢ A Q J 10 9
♣ 10 8

West
♠ Q 10 8 5 2
♡ K 10 2
♢ 2
♣ A K Q 9

East
♠ 6
♡ 5 4
♢ 8 7 6 5 3
♣ J 7 5 3 2

South
♠ A J 9 7 4
♡ A 9 8 3
♢ K 4
♣ 6 4

1. Declarer has either five or six spades along with four hearts and precisely two clubs (partner's count signal at trick one has clarified that suit).
2. If declarer has six spades it is right to return a spade and give partner an immediate ruff. In fact, when he returns a club you can give him another ruff.

   However, if declarer is 5–4–2–2, you must switch to your diamond. Upon winning the ♡K, you must underlead your ♣AK over to partner's hoped-for ♣J and get a diamond ruff. Which is better?

   South gave some thought to passing the double; at this vulnerability it would have been easy to pass with six spades so it is more likely that declarer has five spades. Go for your ruff and lead the ♢2.

KEY LESSON POINTERS

1. IT CAN'T BE EMPHASIZED ENOUGH HOW IMPORTANT IT IS TO WORK OUT DECLARER'S DISTRIBUTION EARLY IN THE PLAY.
2. OPPONENT'S PAUSES AT THE TABLE ARE EXTREMELY REVEALING, AND MANY TIMES YOU CAN HARDLY HELP BUT MAKE INFERENCES FROM WHAT YOU DON'T HEAR.

(20) WHAT A PLEASURE

East-West vulnerable
Dealer South

North
♠ 6 4
♡ J 9 8
◇ K Q 9 7 6
♣ K Q 3

West (you)
♠ K 9 8 7 3
♡ 7 6 3
◇ 2
♣ 10 7 6 5

South	West	North	East
1 ♡	Pass	2 ◇	Pass
2 NT*	Pass	3 ♡	Pass
4 ♡	All Pass		

*15–17

Opening lead: ◇2

Dummy plays low and partner wins the ◇A, declarer playing the ◇J. At trick two partner returns the ◇8. Declarer plays the ◇10 which you ruff.

1. What do you return at this point? Why?

WHAT A PLEASURE (Solution)

North
♠ 6 4
♡ J 9 8
◇ K Q 9 7 6
♣ K Q 3

West
♠ K 9 8 7 3
♡ 7 6 3
◇ 2
♣ 10 7 6 5

East
♠ A 10 5
♡ 5 2
◇ A 8 5 4 3
♣ J 8 4

South
♠ Q J 2
♡ A K Q 10 4
◇ J 10
♣ A 9 2

1. The ♠K. Partner has politely informed you that he has the ♠A with his return of the ◇8, his highest diamond. Now it is your turn to return the favor. If you lazily play a low spade, partner may decide to promote a possible trump queen for you by returning another diamond. If he does that, you lose your ♠K.

KEY LESSON POINTERS

1. THE PLAYER WHO CAN "SEE" THE RIGHT DEFENSE IS THE ONE WHO SHOULD TAKE CHARGE.
2. DO NOT FORGET MURPHY'S LAW: IF THERE IS ANY WAY FOR PARTNER TO GO WRONG, HE WILL.

(21) THE BIKINI NOTRUMP

East-West vulnerable
Dealer South

North
♠ 6 5 3
♡ 10 5 2
◇ A J 3
♣ K 8 6 5

West (you)
♠ A Q 10 9
♡ A Q 3
◇ 7 4
♣ Q J 10 2

South	West	North	East
1 NT*	Dbl.	All Pass	
*10 – 12			

Opening lead: ♣Q

South wins the ♣A, partner playing the ♣3. At trick two declarer leads the ◇6 to the ◇J and partner's ◇K (you play the ◇7).

Partner returns the ♡J. Declarer plays low.

1. Which heart do you play? Why?
2. You play low, partner continues with the ♡8, and declarer plays low again. Which heart do you play this time? Why? What is your plan?
3. You play the ♡A and return the ♡Q to partner's ♡K, declarer following. Partner now plays the thirteenth heart, declarer discarding the ♣7. What do you discard? Why?

THE BIKINI NOTRUMP (Solution)

North
♠ 6 5 3
♡ 10 5 2
♢ A J 3
♣ K 8 6 5

West
♠ A Q 10 9
♡ A Q 3
♢ 7 4
♣ Q J 10 2

East
♠ 8 7 4 2
♡ K J 9 8
♢ K 10 9
♣ 9 3

South
♠ K J
♡ 7 6 4
♢ Q 8 6 5 2
♣ A 7 4

1. The ♡3. Partner may be leading from J98x hoping declarer ducks with Kxx. (Declarer will duck if he thinks East is sneakily leading from a QJ9 combination.)
2. The ♡A. Now you know your partner has the ♡K. If partner had J8x, declarer would have covered the ♡K holding K9xx. If partner had J98x, his second lead would be his lowest card. Therefore, partner has led the jack from a KJ98 combination and you should unblock and return the suit.
3. The ♣2, in order to get a spade shift. (Had you wanted a club continuation you would have discarded a spade.)

KEY LESSON POINTERS

1. WHEN PARTNER LEADS THE QUEEN VS. NOTRUMP, THIRD HAND SIGNALS COUNT IF ONE OR TWO HIGH HONORS REMAIN IN DUMMY AFTER DUMMY HAS PLAYED. THIS HAND IS A COMMON SENSE EXCEPTION, BECAUSE THIRD HAND CANNOT AFFORD TO SPARE THE ♣9. IF THERE WERE NO HONORS IN DUMMY ORIGINALLY, OR NO HONORS REMAINING AFTER DUMMY HAS PLAYED, THIRD HAND SIGNALS ATTITUDE.
2. ALLOW FOR PARTNER TO MAKE "SURROUNDING PLAYS" WHEN THE DUMMY TO YOUR LEFT HAS SOMETHING LIKE 10x, 10xx, 9x, OR 9xx. IN THOSE CASES IT IS RIGHT FOR PARTNER TO LEAD THE JACK FROM KJ9 COMBINATIONS AND THE TEN FROM Q108 COMBINATIONS.
3. VS. NOTRUMP, WHEN FACED WITH A CHOICE OF DISCARDS FROM ONE OF TWO SUITS (PARTNER NOW ON LEAD), DISCARD FROM THE SUIT YOU DO NOT WANT PARTNER TO LEAD, RETAINING BOTH LENGTH AND STRENGTH IN THE SUIT YOU DO WANT LED.

(22) FLANNERY TWO DIAMONDS

North-South vulnerable
Dealer West

North
♠ A 9 8 5
♡ 4
◊ K J 10 3
♣ 9 8 6 3

East (you)
♠ J 7 3
♡ A J 8 6 2
◊ 9 8 7 5
♣ 7

West	North	East	South
2 ◊*	Pass	3 ♡	4 ♣
Pass	4 ♡	Pass	5 ♣
All Pass			

*Four spades and five hearts with 11–15 high card points

Opening lead: ♡K

1. Which heart do you play? Why?

FLANNERY TWO DIAMONDS (Solution)

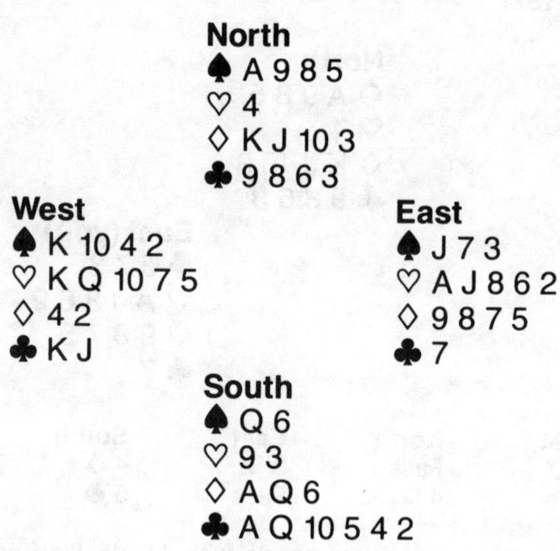

Declarer is known to hold doubletons in each major and should have at least six clubs for his vulnerable four level intervention. Therefore, South is either 2–2–3–6 or 2–2–2–7.

In either case South is going to work with those diamonds to discard any losing spade. You must overtake and switch to a low spade hoping partner has the ♠K10 along with the ◊A or a trump trick. You have no other alternative.

KEY LESSON POINTERS

1. USE THE DISTRIBUTION YOU KNOW ABOUT PARTNER'S HAND TO WORK OUT DECLARER'S DISTRIBUTION.
2. WHEN THERE IS A THREATENING SIDE SUIT IN THE DUMMY, AN ATTACKING, AGGRESSIVE DEFENSE IS USUALLY CALLED FOR.
3. SOMETIMES THE SUIT THAT MUST BE ATTACKED CAN BE ATTACKED ONLY FROM YOUR SIDE OF THE TABLE. IN THAT CASE, IT IS ON YOUR HEAD TO OVERTAKE PARTNER'S WINNER.

(23) TOO MANY GUNS

North-South vulnerable
Dealer South

North
♠ K 3
♡ K Q 6 4
◇ 4
♣ J 10 9 8 7 6

West (you)
♠ Q 9
♡ 5
◇ A J 10 9 3
♣ A Q 5 4 3

South	West	North	East
1 NT	2 NT*	3 ♣**	Pass
3 ♡	Pass	4 ♡	All Pass

*Minors
**Stayman

Opening lead: ♡5

Partner's ♡J drives out the ♡A.

1. What is the trump position?

   Declarer leads a trump to dummy, as you discard a low diamond, and leads a club. Partner discards the ♠2, declarer plays the ♣K.
2. What do you make of declarer's distribution?
3. Do you take this trick? If so, what do you return? If not, why not?

TOO MANY GUNS (Solution)

North
♠ K 3
♡ K Q 6 4
♢ 4
♣ J 10 9 8 7 6

West
♠ Q 9
♡ 5
♢ A J 10 9 3
♣ A Q 5 4 3

East
♠ J 8 7 5 4 2
♡ J 9 3 2
♢ 8 5 2
♣ —

South
♠ A 10 6
♡ A 10 8 7
♢ K Q 7 6
♣ K 2

1. Declarer started with ♡A10xx.
2. Declarer is known to hold four hearts and two clubs. His other two suits are likely divided 4–3 as it would be unusual to open one notrump with a 5-4-2-2 distribution.
   South is more likely to hold three spades and four diamonds than vice versa as partner might have entered the fray with 3♢ with a four card suit at this vulnerability.
3. Win the trick and return a low club allowing partner to ruff. Assuming partner exits with his last trump, declarer will wind up a trick short. Count tricks. After two rounds of trumps have been played, declarer can take no more than six trump tricks (assuming he crossruffs), one diamond and two spades. Your defense requires partner to hold the ♠J, no more. (Even if declarer has the ♠J he will probably finesse into you, the hand short in spades, as he needs three spade tricks to make his contract.)

KEY LESSON POINTERS

1. THERE IS NO SUBSTITUTE FOR COUNTING TRICKS.
2. GIVING PARTNER A RUFF IN DUMMY'S LONG SUIT WHILE STILL RETAINING CONTROL IS AN EFFECTIVE METHOD OF SILENCING THE SUIT.
3. ASSUME WHEN AN OPPONENT OPENS ONE NOTRUMP HE HAS 4–3–3–3, 4–4–3–2, OR 5–3–3–2 DISTRIBUTION. 5–4–2–2 OR 6–3–2–2 HAND PATTERNS ARE TOO EXCEPTIONAL TO WORRY ABOUT.

(24) LOOKING FOR FIVE

North-South vulnerable
Dealer North

North
♠ 9 2
♡ A Q J 9
◊ K Q J 9 4
♣ K Q

East (you)
♠ A J 8 7 6
♡ 7 3 2
◊ A 6
♣ J 10 3

North	East	South	West
1 ◊	1 ♠	1 NT	Pass
3 NT	All Pass		

Opening lead: ♠10

1. What do you play at trick one?
   You win the ♠A.
2. What do you play at trick two?
   You shift to the ♣J, partner winning the ♣A and returning the ♣2.
3. Which club do you play at trick three, and why?

LOOKING FOR FIVE (Solution)

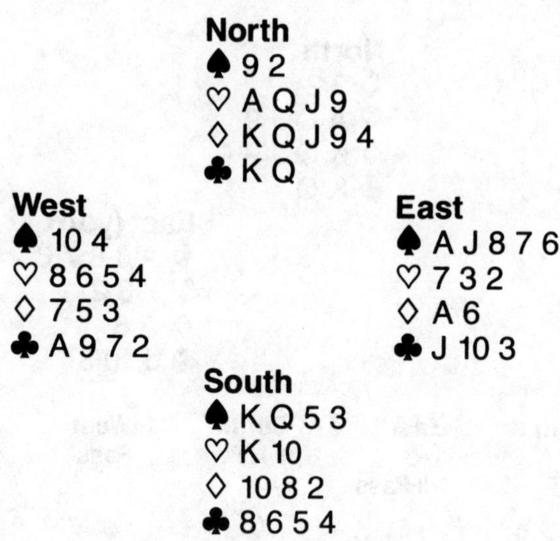

You know that declarer holds two spade stoppers, partner a doubleton, and that your side entry is going to be removed early. This does not augur well for spade establishment. You should look elsewhere.

Clubs seem your best "elsewhere" bet and you must develop at least three tricks before your ♢A is removed. In order to score at least three club tricks, partner needs A9xxx or A97x. In both cases you must unblock the ♣10 on partner's club return.

KEY LESSON POINTERS

1. WHEN YOU DO NOT HAVE ENOUGH TIME OR ENTRIES TO SET UP YOUR OWN SUIT, TRY TO SET UP PARTNER'S.
2. DO NOT HESITATE TO UNBLOCK HIGH HONORS FROM SHORT SUIT HOLDINGS IF THAT IS THE ONLY WAY TO DEFEAT THE CONTRACT.

(25) ONE KING RIGHT AND ONE KING WRONG

Neither side vulnerable
Dealer South

North
♠ 9 2
♡ Q J 3
♢ A Q 9 8
♣ J 5 4 3

East (you)
♠ A 5 4 3
♡ 10 9 2
♢ K 6 2
♣ K 8 2

South	West	North	East
1 ♣	Pass	1 ♢	Pass
3 ♣	Pass	3 ♡	Pass
4 ♢	Pass	5 ♣	All Pass

Opening lead: ♠Q

You win the ♠A and declarer follows with the ♠K.

1. What do you think declarer's distribution is?
2. How do you place the missing high cards around the table?
3. What do you return at trick two?

ONE KING RIGHT AND ONE KING WRONG (Solution)

North
♠ 9 2
♡ Q J 3
◊ A Q 9 8
♣ J 5 4 3

West
♠ Q J 10 8 7 6
♡ 8 6 5 4
◊ 5 4 3
♣ —

East
♠ A 5 4 3
♡ 10 9 2
◊ K 6 2
♣ K 8 2

South
♠ K
♡ A K 7
◊ J 10 7
♣ A Q 10 9 7 6

1. Declarer must be 1–3–3–6. With four hearts he would have bid the suit and with four diamonds he would have raised the suit directly.
2. Declarer must have the missing heart and club honors to justify his jump rebid. Also, partner is known to have ♠QJ10xxx. With a heart honor, wouldn't he have made some noise? Either player can hold the ◊J.
3. The ◊2. Maybe you can con declarer into thinking you have a singleton diamond and talk him out of the club finesse. If you can pull this bit of chicanery off, you will make both of your kings. In any event, your diamond shift cannot cost, as declarer is marked with three diamonds.

KEY LESSON POINTERS

1. WHEN A SILENT PARTNER TURNS UP WITH A LONG, FAIRLY STRONG SUIT, IT IS SAFE TO ASSUME THAT HE HAS NO OUTSIDE ACES OR KINGS.
2. EACH BID THE DECLARER MAKES OR DOESN'T MAKE GIVES A CLUE TO HIS DISTRIBUTION AND HIGH CARD STRENGTH. LISTEN.
3. TRICKING DECLARER INTO THINKING A SIDE SUIT FINESSE IS WORKING, AND THAT HE IS BEING THREATENED BY A RUFF IS ONE WAY OF TALKING HIM OUT OF TAKING A WINNING TRUMP FINESSE.

(26) QUE PASA?

East-West vulnerable
Dealer North

North
♠ K Q 8 6
♡ Q 8
◇ Q J 8
♣ A K 3 2

West (you)
♠ 4 3
♡ A J 6 3 2
◇ 9 5
♣ 10 8 7 4

North	East	South	West
1 NT	3 ◇	3 ♠*	Pass
4 ♠	All Pass		

*Forcing

Opening lead: ◇9

Dummy covers and partner wins the ◇A. At trick two partner shifts to the ♡K.

1. Which heart do you play?
2. You signal with the ♡6 and partner continues with the ♡4, declarer playing the ♡7 and the ♡10. What do you play now?

QUE PASA? (Solution)

North
♠ K Q 8 6
♡ Q 8
◊ Q J 8
♣ A K 3 2

West
♠ 4 3
♡ A J 6 3 2
◊ 9 5
♣ 10 8 7 4

East
♠ 7 2
♡ K 9 5 4
◊ A K 10 7 4 3 2
♣ —

South
♠ A J 10 9 5
♡ 10 7
◊ 6
♣ Q J 9 6 5

Some strange things are going on around here. First, the diamond suit. If partner's play at trick one is for real, partner came storming in at the three level, vulnerable vs. not, on an A10xxxx suit!

Next, the heart suit. Does partner really have ♡K4? If so, where is the setting trick coming from? There is an explanation. Partner must want a *club* shift. He won the ◊A rather than the ◊K in order to discourage you from continuing diamonds should you regain the lead.

Partner knows you must have the ♡A to defeat this contract, and accordingly plays the ♡K.

Furthermore, the play of the ♡K has the advantage of discovering whether you have a singleton diamond. If you do, a player of your stature would surely play a low heart.

On lead with the ♡A, return a club. A heart return can hardly be right. Partner cannot have more than two spades. If one of them is the ♠J and declarer happens to hold ♠A109xx ♡109xx ◊Kx ♣xx, he might go wrong. However, that means partner overcalled 3◊, vulnerable, holding ♠Jx ♡Kx ◊A10xxxx ♣QJx! Are you buying that?

KEY LESSON POINTERS

1. WHEN HOLDING THE AK OF YOUR BID SUIT, WIN THE OPENING LEAD WITH THE ACE IF YOU WANT YOUR PARTNER TO RETURN A DIFFERENT SUIT SHOULD HE REGAIN THE LEAD.
2. WHEN PARTNER LEADS THE KING OF A SUIT IN WHICH YOU HAVE THE ACE, SIGNAL ENCOURAGEMENT IF YOU WANT THE SUIT CONTINUED. IF YOU WANT A SHIFT, PLAY LOW.
3. WHEN YOU HAVE A CHOICE BETWEEN TWO LINES OF DEFENSE, GO BACK TO THE BIDDING AND ASK YOURSELF WHICH HAND PARTNER IS MORE LIKELY TO HOLD.

(27) GOOD TRUMPS

Neither side vulnerable
Dealer South

North
♠ Q J
♡ J 8 7
◊ Q J 6 4 3
♣ Q 10 9

East (you)
♠ 7 3 2
♡ A K 3 2
◊ K 10 9 5
♣ 8 3

South	West	North	East
1 ♡	Pass	2 ♡	Pass
4 ♡	All Pass		

Opening lead: ♠10 (Denies a higher honor when the jack is visible.)

Dummy's jack holds. At trick two the ♡7 is led from dummy which also holds when you duck, partner playing the ♡4. At trick three the ♡8 goes to your king, partner discarding the ♣4. Now what?

GOOD TRUMPS (Solution)

North
♠ Q J
♡ J 8 7
◇ Q J 6 4 3
♣ Q 10 9

West
♠ 10 9 8 6
♡ 4
◇ A 8 7
♣ J 7 6 5 4

East
♠ 7 3 2
♡ A K 3 2
◇ K 10 9 5
♣ 8 3

South
♠ A K 5 4
♡ Q 10 9 6 5
◇ 2
♣ A K 2

Judging from the lead and partner's discard of a low club, your best bet is to play partner for the ◇A. Even so, a certain amount of TLC is required.

For example, if you were to lead a low diamond to partner's ace and he returned the suit, dummy would cover, your king would be ruffed, and declarer could concede another trump trick, period.

But what if you play the ◇K? Now when you continue the suit, declarer must ruff reducing to your trump length. When you get in with your remaining trump honor, you can play another diamond. If declarer ruffs, you have the outstanding trump; if declarer discards, partner wins the ◇A for the setting trick.

KEY LESSON POINTERS

1. TWO QUICK TRUMP TRICKS WITH FOUR TRUMPS IS A POWERFUL DEFENSIVE WEAPON.
   YOUR OBJECTIVE SHOULD BE TO EITHER SECURE A RUFF OR FORCE DECLARER TO RUFF ONCE OR TWICE TO PROMOTE ONE OF YOUR TINY TRUMPS TO A LONG SUIT WINNER.
2. WHEN CONTEMPLATING THE FORCING GAME HOLDING Kxx OR Kxxx WITH THE DUMMY TO YOUR RIGHT HOLDING QJx, QJxx, OR QJxxx, IT CAN BE SO RIGHT TO BEGIN WITH THE KING IF PARTNER HAS THE ACE. IF DECLARER HAS A SINGLETON YOU WILL BE ABLE TO FORCE HIM TO RUFF TWICE WITHOUT SETTING UP A WINNER IN THE DUMMY.

(28) WAY AHEAD

Both sides vulnerable
Dealer South

North
♠ 10 4
♡ K Q 8 7 6
◊ A 10 6 4
♣ A Q

East (you)
♠ A K 9
♡ 3 2
◊ 7 3 2
♣ K J 7 6 5

South	West	North	East
2 ♠*	Pass	4 ♠	All Pass

*Weak (7–10 high card points—six card suit)

Opening lead: ♡10

1. What is your initial reaction to the heart distribution? Declarer wins the ♡J, as you begin a tiny echo with the ♡3. At trick two declarer leads the ♠2 to the ♠10.
2. What do you think the spade position is?
3. Where do you place the missing diamond honors?
4. What is your plan?

WAY AHEAD (Solution)

North
♠ 10 4
♡ K Q 8 7 6
◊ A 10 6 4
♣ A Q

West
♠ 5 3
♡ 10 9 5
◊ K J 8 5
♣ 8 4 3 2

East
♠ A K 9
♡ 3 2
◊ 7 3 2
♣ K J 7 6 5

South
♠ Q J 8 7 6 2
♡ A J 4
◊ Q 9
♣ 10 9

1. Partner probably has a three card suit. If partner has a doubleton, declarer has opened a vulnerable weak two bid with a marginal six card spade suit holding ♡AJxx. Hardly.
   If partner has four hearts, he might have led low. Furthermore, if declarer had ♡AJ doubleton he would surely have won the opening lead with the ace to avoid blocking the suit. True, if partner had 1098x or 1097x of hearts he would have led the ten, but you can see the ♡8 and ♡7 in dummy.
2. Six spades to the queen-jack. What else?
3. Partner probably has the ◊K J and declarer the ◊Q. If declarer had the ◊K he would have opened 1♠. If partner had the ◊K Q he would have led the suit.
4. Your plan should be to go for a heart ruff. Win the ♠K and exit with your remaining heart. Declarer will win and play a spade. You will win and return a diamond, locking declarer in dummy. No matter how declarer wriggles he cannot stop your partner from getting in to give you a heart ruff. Sorry, but you don't make your ♣K. If partner plays a club instead of a heart, you get neither the ♣K nor the ruff!

KEY LESSON POINTERS

1. WHEN PARTNER LEADS A TEN AND THE EIGHT, OR, BETTER, THE EIGHT AND SEVEN ARE BOTH VISIBLE, CHANCES ARE THAT PARTNER IS LEADING FROM A DOUBLETON OR 109x.
2. WHEN THE KING AND QUEEN (OR ACE AND KING) OF A SIDE SUIT ARE NOT VISIBLE IN EITHER DUMMY OR YOUR HAND (IN BACK OF DUMMY), ASSUME THAT THE HONORS ARE SPLIT OR THAT DECLARER HAS THEM BOTH.
3. THE CARD THAT DECLARER USES TO WIN A TRICK (WHEN HOLDING EQUALS) CAN BE VERY REVEALING.

(29) SINGLETON RAISE

Neither side vulnerable
Dealer South

North
♠ Q 8 7 6
♡ 3
♢ Q 7
♣ A K 9 8 7 6

East (you)
♠ J 10 9 2
♡ 4 2
♢ A 8 6
♣ 10 4 3 2

South	West	North	East
2 ♣*	Pass	3 ♣	Pass
3 ♡	Pass	4 ♣	Pass
4 ♡	Pass	5 ♡	Pass
6 ♡	All Pass		

*Strong and artificial

Opening lead: ♢2

Dummy plays low, plan your defense.

SINGLETON RAISE (Solution)

North
♠ Q 8 7 6
♡ 3
◇ Q 7
♣ A K 9 8 7 6

West
♠ K 5 4 3
♡ 6 5
◇ J 5 3 2
♣ Q J 5

East
♠ J 10 9 2
♡ 4 2
◇ A 8 6
♣ 10 4 3 2

South
♠ A
♡ A K Q J 10 9 8 7
◇ K 10 9 4
♣ —

Declarer is known to hold the ◇K and the ♠A from the bidding. North was unable to cue bid either of those suits so South must have those controls.

The lead has indicated that South has four diamonds, and the bidding has indicated that South has seven or eight hearts.

Therefore, there is an excellent chance that South is void in clubs and the defense must keep South from getting to dummy.

To do this, you must play the ◇8 at trick one! If a diamond is returned, win and return a trump. If your analysis is correct partner will eventually make a second diamond trick if he started with Jxxx or 109xx.

Even if declarer does have a club you will not lose your ◇A. You cannot lose by playing the ◇8.

KEY LESSON POINTERS

1. IF YOU SUSPECT DECLARER IS VOID IN DUMMY'S LONG STRONG SUIT, YOUR DEFENSE SHOULD BE ORIENTED TO KEEP DECLARER FROM GETTING TO DUMMY.
2. THIRD HAND SOMETIMES HAS TO MAKE SOME RATHER UNUSUAL PLAYS TO PREVENT DECLARER FROM GETTING TO DUMMY.

(30) YOUR TURN

Both sides vulnerable
Dealer South

North
♠ K 9 8 4
♡ A K Q 10
♢ Q 3
♣ 7 6 5

East (you)
♠ Q 6
♡ 9 8 7 5
♢ 9 8 7 5 4
♣ 4 2

South	West	North	East
1 ♢	3 ♣*	Dbl.**	Pass
3 ♠	Pass	4 ♠	All Pass

*Weak
**Negative

Opening lead: ♣K

Partner continues with the ♣A dropping declarer's ♣Q, and at trick three continues with the ♣8.

1. What card do you play to this trick? Why?

YOUR TURN (Solution)

North
♠ K 9 8 4
♡ A K Q 10
♢ Q 3
♣ 7 6 5

West
♠ J 10 7
♡ 6 3 2
♢ 10
♣ A K J 10 9 8

East
♠ Q 6
♡ 9 8 7 5
♢ 9 8 7 5 4
♣ 4 2

South
♠ A 5 3 2
♡ J 4
♢ A K J 6 2
♣ Q 3

1. The ♠6. Your partner clearly wants you to trump this trick; otherwise he would have played the ♣J, a card he is known to hold.

   In situations like this, it is usually right to trump with your HIGHEST trump, an "uppercut", to promote partner's trump holding. However, in this case you can see that regardless of which three trumps partner has, ruffing with the ♠Q won't help. Declarer will overtrump and lead a spade to the nine. If partner splits his honors, dummy wins and the remaining trump honor is forced out to score the game.

   As this is a desperate situation, you must play for the one trump holding in partner's hand that can help you, namely, ♠J 10 7. In that case you can trump with the ♠6 and promote two trump tricks for your side. Desperate players make desperate plays.

KEY LESSON POINTERS

1. WHEN PARTNER KNOWS YOU ARE VOID IN A SUIT AND LEADS LOW (WHEN YOU KNOW HE HOLDS THE MASTER CARDS IN THE SUIT) HE WANTS YOU TO RUFF AS HIGH AS POSSIBLE. THIS HAND IS AN EXCEPTION.
2. WHEN ONLY ONE COMBINATION ALLOWS YOU TO DEFEAT A CONTRACT, PLAY FOR IT.

(31) THE GUIDING LIGHT

Both sides vulnerable
Dealer South

North
♠ K J 8 7
♡ A Q 7 2
◇ K 6 5
♣ 7 4

East (you)
♠ 4 2
♡ K 10 8
◇ A Q 9 3
♣ K 10 6 5

South	**West**	**North**	**East**
1 ◇	Pass	1 ♡	Pass
1 ♠	Pass	4 ♠	All Pass

Opening lead: ◇2

1. What is declarer's distribution in diamonds and spades?
2. What are the relevant distributions in the other suits?
3. Who has the ♣A?
4. Dummy plays low and you win the ◇Q. What do you play at trick two?

THE GUIDING LIGHT (Solution)

North
♠ K J 8 7
♡ A Q 7 2
◊ K 6 5
♣ 7 4

West
♠ 6 5 3
♡ J 9 6 5 4
◊ 2
♣ Q 9 3 2

East
♠ 4 2
♡ K 10 8
◊ A Q 9 3
♣ K 10 6 5

South
♠ A Q 10 9
♡ 3
◊ J 10 8 7 4
♣ A J 8

1. Five diamonds and four spades judging from the obvious singleton lead in declarer's first bid suit.
2. As you can always cash two diamonds and give partner a diamond ruff, declarer will have no chance if he started with two or three hearts, so don't worry about those distributions. Problems arise when declarer has a singleton heart. If you play three rounds of diamonds, declarer, after drawing trumps, will discard a losing club from dummy on an established diamond.
3. South, unless he has decided to open first hand, vulnerable, with ♠AQxx ♡J ◊J10xxx ♣QJx.
4. The ◊3. This caters to everything. Your partner gets his ruff, and you retain control of the suit. After partner ruffs and switches to a club as you have requested, declarer has no chance.

KEY LESSON POINTERS

1. GIVING PARTNER A RUFF IS NOT ALWAYS THE ANSWER. IF YOU SET UP A VALUABLE DISCARD, OR DISCARDS, FOR DECLARER THE PLAY CAN BE COSTLY. IF POSSIBLE TRY TO RETAIN CONTROL OF DECLARER'S SIDE SUIT WHILE GIVING A RUFF.
2. WHEN TRYING TO WORK OUT DECLARER'S POSSIBLE DISTRIBUTIONS, CONCENTRATE ON THE RELEVANT ONES.

(32) LIGHT JUMP SHIFT

East-West vulnerable
Dealer North

North
♠ K 6 5 3
♡ 8
♢ A K 10 9 3 2
♣ A K

West (you)
♠ A 10 2
♡ A 9 7 6 5
♢ J 7
♣ Q 10 9

North	East	South	West
1 ♢	Pass	1 ♡	Pass
2 ♠	Pass	2 NT	Pass
3 NT	All Pass		

Opening lead: ♡6

Partner produces the ♡10 which loses to the ♡Q. At trick two South leads the ♠8.

1. Why do you think South is leading spades instead of diamonds?
2. Which spade do you play? What is your plan?

LIGHT JUMP SHIFT (Solution)

North
♠ K 6 5 3
♡ 8
◊ A K 10 9 3 2
♣ A K

West
♠ A 10 2
♡ A 9 7 6 5
◊ J 7
♣ Q 10 9

East
♠ Q 9 4
♡ 10 4 3
◊ Q 8 6
♣ 8 7 5 3

South
♠ J 8 7
♡ K Q J 2
◊ 5 4
♣ J 6 4 2

1. Because South is in his hand for the last time and has to lead up to the ♠K to realize nine tricks.
2. The ♠A, and return a low heart. Partner must have a diamond trick, or else you are playing for drill. If partner has a diamond trick, you want your hearts to be established when partner gets in.

   If you duck the spade, dummy will win and declarer will switch to diamonds before your hearts are established. By the way, you don't need partner to hold the ♡J; any three hearts will do.

KEY LESSON POINTERS

1. WHEN DECLARER SEEMINGLY ABANDONS A LONG STRONG SUIT AT NOTRUMP, THERE ARE A NUMBER OF POSSIBLE REASONS:
   (a) THE MOST LIKELY IS THAT DECLARER HAS THE MISSING HONOR(S);
   (b) DECLARER MUST USE HIS HAND ENTRY (ENTRIES?) FOR MORE IMPORTANT PURPOSES;
   (c) DECLARER HAS A BETTER SUIT TO WORK WITH.
   (d) DECLARER IS STEALING.

2. WHEN IT IS APPARENT THAT THE HAND CANNOT BE DEFEATED UNLESS PARTNER HAS A CERTAIN CARD OR CARDS, ASSUME HE HAS THOSE CARDS AND PLAY ACCORDINGLY.
3. CONTRARILY, IF A CERTAIN CARD IS NOT NEEDED IN PARTNER'S HAND, DO NOT "HOPE" HE HAS IT. FOR EXAMPLE, ON THIS HAND PARTNER DOES NOT NEED THE ♡J. TRUE, IF PARTNER HAS ♡J10x YOU CAN DEFEAT THE HAND AN EXTRA TRICK BY NOT LEADING THE SUIT, BUT IT INVOLVES A RISK YOU NEED NOT TAKE.

(33) A TRUE FRIEND

Neither side vulnerable
Dealer North

North
♠ A J 7 2
♡ J 5
◊ 5 4 3 2
♣ A K Q

East (you)
♠ 9 4
♡ K 10 8 7 4
◊ A 6
♣ 8 7 3 2

North	**East**	**South**	**West**
1 ♣	Pass	1 ♡	Pass
1 ♠	Pass	2 NT*	Pass
3 NT	All Pass		

*Not forcing

Opening lead: ◊ 7

1. How many diamonds does partner have?
   You win the ◊A and return the suit to partner's king, declarer playing the nine and queen. Partner exits with the ◊8 as you discard a low club. Declarer wins the ◊J and leads the ♠6. Partner plays the ♠5 and dummy's ♠J wins the trick.
2. The ♡J is led from dummy. Do you cover?
   If you wish to continue in the game, you cover. Declarer plays low and partner plays the ♡9.
3. What is declarer's probable distribution?
4. What do you play at this point? Why?

A TRUE FRIEND (Solution)

North
♠ A J 7 2
♡ J 5
◊ 5 4 3 2
♣ A K Q

West
♠ K 10 8 5
♡ 9
◊ K 10 8 7
♣ J 9 6 5

East
♠ 9 4
♡ K 10 8 7 4
◊ A 6
♣ 8 7 3 2

South
♠ Q 6 3
♡ A Q 6 3 2
◊ Q J 9
♣ 10 4

1. Four, because he has led his lowest diamond.
2. Yes, because you have promotable spot cards.
3. 3–5–3–2. Declarer is known to have three diamonds and partner's play of the ♡9 suggests a singleton. (It would be too risky to play the ♡9 from a doubleton as it could expose you to a finesse if declarer started with AQ8x(x)). The bidding and the play suggest that partner has four spades.
4. A spade. Declarer has eight sure tricks, three clubs, two hearts, two spades plus one diamond. You must assume partner has the ♠K10 or else there is no hope. If partner has those cards you must return a spade or else declarer will strip partner of his clubs after cashing two hearts, and throw partner in with a diamond, forcing a spade lead away from his king.

KEY LESSON POINTERS

1. A STRONG PARTNER WILL NOT SIGNAL HIGH-LOW WITH TWO (OR FOUR) CARDS IF THE SPOT CARD CAN CONCEIVABLY WIN A TRICK OR EXPOSE EITHER PLAYER TO A LATER FINESSE. (WEST'S PLAY OF THE ♠5).
2. KEEPING TRACK OF DECLARER'S POINT COUNT, DISTRIBUTION, AND TRICKS ENABLES YOU TO MAKE SOME STRONG PLAYS, SUCH AS GETTING PARTNER OFF OF AN ENDPLAY.

(34) WHAT IS HE TRYING TO TELL ME?

Both sides vulnerable
Dealer South

North
♠ J 10 9 6
♡ A K J 10 3
♢ 10
♣ 7 6 5

West (you)
♠ 7 3 2
♡ 9 7 6 4 2
♢ 9 5 3
♣ A K

South	West	North	East
1 ♢	Pass	1 ♡	Pass
1 ♠	Pass	3 ♠	Pass
4 ♠	All Pass		

Opening lead: ♣A

Partner plays the ♣9 and declarer the ♣4. You continue with the ♣K and partner plays the ♣J and declarer the ♣8.

1. What do you play to trick three?

WHAT IS HE TRYING TO TELL ME? (Solution)

North
♠ J 10 9 6
♡ A K J 10 3
◇ 10
♣ 7 6 5

West
♠ 7 3 2
♡ 9 7 6 4 2
◇ 9 5 3
♣ A K

East
♠ A 5
♡ 8 5
◇ Q J 6 4
♣ J 10 9 3 2

South
♠ K Q 8 4
♡ Q
◇ A K 8 7 2
♣ Q 8 4

1. A trump! When you led the ♣A, partner did not know you had the ♣K and was signalling encouragement. Two reasons for signalling high without the ♣K are (1) the ♣QJ; (2) a quick trump entry, anticipating a ruff.

   When you continue with the ♣K, partner learns that you started with a doubleton and his second card is suit preference. Can partner be void in hearts? Hardly. Would partner have signalled encouragement in clubs if he wanted a heart shift? No, partner is not void in hearts, nor does he have the ◇A. Had he the ◇A, his second club would have been his smallest, not his biggest.

   As there is a real danger that declarer has both the ◇AK and will discard a club from dummy if a trump is not led to partner's ace, that is the play you must make at once. It isn't just any player who will try for a ruff by leading a trump. You are really something else!

KEY LESSON POINTERS

1. WHEN YOU LEAD THE ACE FROM AK DOUBLETON, DON'T EXPECT PARTNER TO BE A MINDREADER. HIS FIRST PLAY IS ATTITUDE. WHEN YOU LATER LEAD THE KING SHOWING A DOUBLETON, HIS SECOND PLAY IS SUIT PREFERENCE.
2. ALTHOUGH ONE DOESN'T USUALLY LEAD A TRUMP WHEN ONE IS LOOKING FOR A RUFF, THIS HAND IS THE EXCEPTION.

(35) PLAYING THE ODDS

Both sides vulnerable
Dealer South

North
♠ A J 10 8 7
♡ 5 3
◊ Q J 10 8 7
♣ Q

West (you)
♠ 9
♡ K 9 8
◊ 3
♣ A K 10 9 8 7 6 5

South	West	North	East
1 ◊	5 ♣*	5 ◊	All Pass

*You don't kid around.

Opening lead: ♣K

Partner plays the ♣3 and declarer the ♣J.

1. What do you lead to trick two?

PLAYING THE ODDS (Solution)

North
♠ A J 10 8 7
♡ 5 3
◊ Q J 10 8 7
♣ Q

West
♠ 9
♡ K 9 8
◊ 3
♣ A K 10 9 8 7 6 5

East
♠ 6 5 4 3 2
♡ A 10 7 6 2
◊ 4
♣ 3 2

South
♠ K Q
♡ Q J 4
◊ A K 9 6 5 2
♣ J 4

1. A heart, preferably the ♡K.

It isn't 100% clear to switch to a heart, but it gains far more often than it loses.

The heart switch wins (the good news), when (1) partner has the ♡A regardless of his spade holding; (2) when partner has the ♡Q and the ♠K. In that case a heart trick must be developed before the spades are established.

The heart switch loses (the bad news), when declarer has ♡AQxx and no honors in spades or ♡AQx along with three small spades.

Lead the ♡K rather than a low heart because your partner might have trouble reading the ♡8. If he holds the ♡A he may decide the best chance to defeat the contract is to try to give you a spade ruff.

KEY LESSON POINTERS

1. MANY TIMES A DEFENDER WITHOUT SUFFICIENT INFORMATION AT HIS DISPOSAL MUST MAKE A CRITICAL SHIFT. HE DOES BEST TO DECIDE ON A PERCENTAGE BASIS WHICH SHIFT IS MORE LIKELY TO WORK. PARTNER WILL UNDERSTAND—AS LONG AS YOU DO THE RIGHT THING.
2. LEADING "LOW" FROM A HIGH HONOR IN A SUIT YOU WANT RETURNED MAY BACKFIRE WHEN YOUR LOW CARD IS RELATIVELY HIGH. FOR ONE THING, PARTNER MAY THINK YOU ARE LOOKING FOR A SWITCH TO ANOTHER SUIT. CONSIDER LEADING THE HONOR.

(36) VULNERABLE GAME

North-South vulnerable
Dealer South

North
♠ A 10 8 7 6 5
♡ J 9
◊ 7 6
♣ Q 9 4

West (you)
♠ K 9 3
♡ 5 4
◊ K Q J 9 8
♣ A 10 5

South	West	North	East
1 ♡	2 ◊	Pass	3 ◊
3 ♡	Pass	4 ♡	All Pass

Opening lead: ◊K

1. East plays the ◊5 and South the ◊10. Is partner's play attitude or count?
2. You continue with a diamond to partner's ace which declarer ruffs. Declarer leads a spade to the ten and partner's jack. Partner switches to the ♣2. Declarer plays the ♣7. Which club do you play? Why?

VULNERABLE GAME (Solution)

North
♠ A 10 8 7 6 5
♡ J 9
◊ 7 6
♣ Q 9 4

West
♠ K 9 3
♡ 5 4
◊ K Q J 9 8
♣ A 10 5

East
♠ Q J
♡ 6 3 2
◊ A 5 4 3 2
♣ J 8 2

South
♠ 4 2
♡ A K Q 10 9 8
◊ 10
♣ K 7 6 3

1. Attitude.
2. The ♣10. Partner does not have the ♣K (declarer needs it to justify his vulnerable bidding). Partner must return a club from any holding to knock out the entry to the spade suit before it becomes established. You must play your partner for ♣J82 or J8xx with the doubleton queen of hearts. In either case, declarer must lose two more club tricks.

KEY LESSON POINTERS

1. WHEN PARTNER LEADS A HIGH HONOR CARD, THIRD HAND USUALLY SIGNALS ATTITUDE. COUNT OR SUIT PREFERENCE SIGNALS ARE THE EXCEPTIONS. COUNT IS GIVEN WHEN THE HONOR HOLDING IS KNOWN, SUIT PREFERENCE WHEN:
   (1) DUMMY HAS A SINGLETON, STRONG TRUMPS AND A POWERFUL SIDE SUIT;
   (2) THIRD HAND HAS BID THE SUIT SHOWING AT LEAST SIX CARDS;
   (3) IT IS TOTALLY OBVIOUS THAT A HIGH CARD CANNOT POSSIBLY ASK FOR A CONTINUATION AND THAT THE PLAYER MAKING THE SIGNAL CANNOT BE SHORTSUITED.
2. USE THE BIDDING TO DETERMINE WHETHER PARTNER OR DECLARER HAS THE MISSING KEY HONORS. IN CLOSE CASES CHECK THE VULNERABILITY. FAVORABLE VULNERABILITY ENCOURAGES PLAYERS TO BID ON THEIR GOOD LOOKS.
3. WHEN DECLARER IS ESTABLISHING A SIDE SUIT, TRY TO REMOVE THE SIDE SUIT ENTRY BEFORE THE SUIT CAN BE ESTABLISHED.

(37) EN GARDE!

East-West vulnerable
Dealer East

North
♠ A K Q 3 2
♡ A K J 10
◇ K
♣ 10 6 5

West (you)
♠ J 9 8
♡ Q 3
◇ Q J 3 2
♣ A 9 7 4

East	South	West	North
3 ◇	Pass	4 ◇	Dbl.
Pass	4 ♠	All Pass	

Opening lead: ◇Q

Partner wins and shifts to the ♣J, declarer covering with the ♣Q. Plan your defense.

EN GARDE! (Solution)

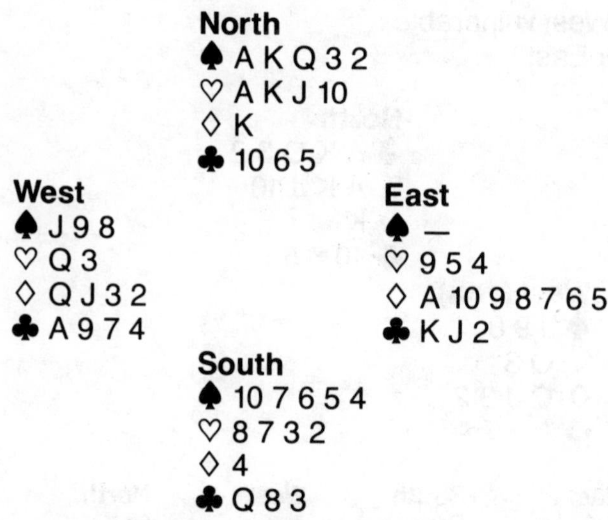

Win the ♣A and exit with a major suit card. There is little point in returning a club. Even if partner ruffs, that is your last trick.

Assume for the moment that partner has a singleton club with 1–4–7–1 distribution. You return a club, dummy plays low, partner ruffs and . . . and that is the end.

The real hope is that partner has led the ♣J from KJx. Why the jack? Keep in mind partner did not know that you had four diamonds. From his point of view, declarer may be able to discard clubs on hearts. His switch caters to you holding either the ♣AQx(x) or the ♣A98(x).

You, on the other hand, know of the singleton diamond in declarer's hand, and at most five spades. In order to defeat the contract, partner must have precisely three clubs, so play partner for ♣KJx. Since you don't know (or care) who has the ♣8, exit safely and wait for your three club tricks.

KEY LESSON POINTERS

1. ALLOW FOR PARTNER TO ATTACK WITH THE JACK FROM AJx OR KJx WHEN 10x, OR 10xx IS IN THE DUMMY TO HIS RIGHT.
2. WHEN TWO POSSIBILITIES PRESENT THEMSELVES, (PARTNER HAVING A SINGLETON CLUB OR KJx), PLAY FOR THE ONE THAT WILL DEFEAT THE CONTRACT.
3. WHEN YOU KNOW MORE ABOUT DECLARER'S DISTRIBUTION THAN PARTNER, IT IS UP TO YOU TO TAKE CHARGE OF THE DEFENSE.

(38) WHOA NELLIE

Both sides vulnerable
Dealer East

North
♠ A
♡ A Q 10
♢ K J 8 7 4
♣ 8 7 4 2

West (you)
♠ J 9 7 6 3 2
♡ 7 5 4
♢ 6
♣ A 10 9

East	South	West	North
Pass	Pass	Pass	1 ♢
Pass	2 NT	Pass	3 NT
All Pass			

Opening lead: ♠6

Partner plays the ♠10 and declarer the ♠5. At trick two declarer crosses to the ♢A, partner playing the ♢3, and leads the ♡6 to the ♡Q and ♡K. At trick four partner cashes the ♠K and declarer plays the ♠8.

1. Which spade do you play? Why?

WHOA NELLIE (Solution)

North
♠ A
♡ A Q 10
◇ K J 8 7 4
♣ 8 7 4 2

West
♠ J 9 7 6 3 2
♡ 7 5 4
◇ 6
♣ A 10 9

East
♠ K 10 4
♡ K 9 8 3
◇ 10 9 3
♣ K J 5

South
♠ Q 8 5
♡ J 6 2
◇ A Q 5 2
♣ Q 6 3

1. The ♠J. To alert your partner that declarer has the ♠Q. By playing the ♠J you deny a higher honor and show the lower equals. The rest is up to partner. If he is on the ball he will shift to a club and you will take three tricks in that suit to defeat the contract.

KEY LESSON POINTERS

1. THE DISCARD OF AN HONOR, OR THE UNBLOCK OF AN HONOR IN A SUIT THAT YOU HAVE PREVIOUSLY LED DENIES A HIGHER HONOR AND SHOWS THE LOWER EQUALS. FOR EXAMPLE:

North (Dummy)
♠ A 9

West
♠ 10 8 7 6 5

East
♠ J 3 2

South
♠ K Q 4

WEST LEADS THE ♠6. NO MATTER HOW THE PLAY DEVELOPS, WEST'S SECOND PLAY IN SPADES SHOULD BE THE ♠10.

North
♠ A 5 4

West
♠ J 9 8 7 6

East
♠ 10 3

South
♠ K Q 2

WEST LEADS THE ♠7, DUMMY PLAYS LOW AND EAST'S TEN DRIVES OUT THE ♠K. NO MATTER HOW THE PLAY DEVELOPS, WEST'S SECOND PLAY IN SPADES SHOULD BE THE ♠J.

(39) SELLING OUT

East-West vulnerable
Dealer West

North
♠ Q J 8 7
♡ A J 5 2
◇ A 8 2
♣ 9 7

West (you)
♠ A K 5
♡ K 9 7 6
◇ K
♣ A J 6 3 2

West	**North**	**East**	**South**
1 ♣	Dbl.	Pass	1 ◇
Dbl.	Pass	1 ♠	2 ◇
All Pass			

Opening lead: ♠K

Partner plays the ♠10 and declarer the ♠6.

1. What do you play to trick two? Why?
2. You return a low heart. Dummy plays low and partner wins the ♡Q, declarer following with the ♡3. Partner returns a low club, declarer plays the ♣10 and you win the ♣J. Now what?

SELLING OUT (Solution)

North
♠ Q J 8 7
♡ A J 5 2
◇ A 8 2
♣ 9 7

West
♠ A K 5
♡ K 9 7 6
◇ K
♣ A J 6 3 2

East
♠ 10 4 3 2
♡ Q 8 4
◇ J 10 7
♣ Q 5 4

South
♠ 9 6
♡ 10 3
◇ Q 9 6 5 4 3
♣ K 10 8

1. Partner's ♠10 reeks of suit preference. After all, he has bid spades and, given dummy's spades, he can hardly want a continuation.
2. Cash your black suit winners and sit back and hope to get a diamond trick. If you fail to cash your spade ace it will go away via a ♡ finesse.

KEY LESSON POINTERS

1. IN GENERAL, WHEN THE KING IS LED AND THE QUEEN APPEARS IN DUMMY, THIRD HAND GIVES COUNT IF HE HAS SUPPORTED THE SUIT, USUALLY BY PLAYING SECOND HIGH FROM FOUR CARDS. HOWEVER, IF THE OPENING LEADER HAS REASON TO BELIEVE THAT THIRD HAND MAY HAVE PLAYED HIS HIGHEST CARD, HE SHOULD ASSUME SUIT PREFERENCE RATHER THAN COUNT.
2. THERE COMES A TIME WHERE YOU HAVE TO CASH YOUR WINNING TRICKS, SIT BACK, AND HOPE SOMETHING GOOD DEVELOPS IN THE TRUMP SUIT.

(40) THE LOVED ONE

East-West vulnerable
Dealer South

North
♠ A K Q 3 2
♡ K J 9 5 2
♢ J
♣ A 3

East (you)
♠ J 10 6 5
♡ 8 4 3
♢ A 9 8 2
♣ K 2

South	West	North	East
4♣	Pass	5♣	All Pass

Opening lead: ♢K

1. Which diamond do you play at trick one? What is your plan?

THE LOVED ONE (Solution)

North
♠ A K Q 3 2
♡ K J 9 5 2
◊ J
♣ A 3

West
♠ 9 7 4
♡ A 10 6
◊ K Q 10 7 4 3
♣ 7

East
♠ J 10 6 5
♡ 8 4 3
◊ A 9 8 2
♣ K 2

South
♠ 8
♡ Q 7
◊ 6 5
♣ Q J 10 9 8 6 5 4

1. Every book of problems has a few insults. This is one. Overtake and return a heart before partner does something foolish like underlead his ♡A at trick two. Remember, you can see the ♣K behind the ace; partner can't.

KEY LESSON POINTERS

1. DON'T ALLOW PARTNER TO HOLD THE LEAD WHEN YOU KNOW HOW TO DEFEAT THE CONTRACT (PARTNER MAY NOT).
2. EVEN EXPERTS MAKE "UNFORTUNATE" PLAYS WHEN THEIR PARTNERS TURN UP WITH UNEXPECTED TRICKS IN UNEXPECTED PLACES.
3. IF YOU WANT TO BE A LOVED AND CHERISHED PARTNER, TAKE YOUR TIME BEFORE PLAYING TO THE FIRST TRICK.

(41) THE SPADES HAVE IT

Neither side vulnerable
Dealer South

North
♠ 9 2
♡ A 7 4
♢ J 10 9 8
♣ 9 4 3 2

East (you)
♠ 4 3
♡ Q J 6 5
♢ A Q 7
♣ 10 8 7 6

South	West	North	East
1 ♠	2 ♣	Pass	3 ♣
3 ♠	Pass	4 ♠*	All Pass

*Sporting raise

Opening lead: ♣Q

Partner's lead is ruffed and declarer plays the ♠A K, partner following with the ♠10 and then the ♠J.

At trick four declarer leads a diamond to the ten, you win with the queen, partner playing the ♢2. Question time.

1. Who has the ♠Q? Why?
2. What is declarer's distribution?
3. What do you play after winning the ♢Q?

THE SPADES HAVE IT (Solution)

	North	
	♠ 9 2	
	♡ A 7 4	
	◇ J 10 9 8	
	♣ 9 4 3 2	
West		**East**
♠ J 10		♠ 4 3
♡ 9 3 2		♡ Q J 6 5
◇ K 6 2		◇ A Q 7
♣ A K Q J 5		♣ 10 8 7 6
	South	
	♠ A K Q 8 7 6 5	
	♡ K 10 8	
	◇ 5 4 3	
	♣ —	

1. Declarer. If partner had ♠QJ10 he would play the ♠Q and then the ♠10, highest-lowest, to let you in on the secret. Also, holding ♠AKxxxx plus a club void, South might have doubled 3♣ for takeout rather than rebidding 3♠.
2. 7–3–3–0 judging from partner's ◇2, a count signal indicating an odd number of diamonds.
3. A low heart. Declarer is known to have seven spade tricks. If declarer has the ◇K, partner must have the ♡K, and the ♡A must be removed before the long diamond is established.

   If partner has the ◇K, then declarer has the ♡K, and again a heart trick must be established before the diamonds are set up.

   If partner has either the ♡K or the ♡10 it doesn't matter which heart you lead, but if declarer has both of those cards you must lead low. There are two critical cases:

   (1) Declarer has K10x and neglects to play the ♡10.

   (2) Declarer has K108. In this case his percentage play is the ♡8, winning whenever you have honor-nine, but losing when you have cleverly underled the QJ.

KEY LESSON POINTERS

1. WHEN YOU HOLD A THREE- OR FOUR-CARD SEQUENCE IN THEIR TRUMP SUIT, PLAY THE HIGHEST AND THEN THE LOWEST IN THAT ORDER.
2. WHEN ATTACKING A SIDE SUIT HOLDING QJxx(x), DUMMY TO YOUR RIGHT, IT IS FREQUENTLY RIGHT TO LEAD LOW, PARTICULARLY WHEN DUMMY HAS EITHER THE ACE OR THE KING AND YOU SUSPECT THE OTHER HIGH HONOR IS IN DECLARER'S HAND.

(42) BLACK DEUCES

Neither side vulnerable
Dealer South

North
♠ K J 4
♡ 9 7 4 3
◊ A 6 3
♣ A 8 6

West (you)
♠ 9 8 3
♡ A 10 2
◊ Q 8 7 5 2
♣ Q 3

South	West	North	East
1 ◊	Pass	1 ♡	Pass
1 NT	Pass	2 NT	Pass
3 NT	All Pass		

Opening lead: ♠9

Declarer plays the ♠K and this is greeted by the ♠2 from partner. At trick two a low diamond is led to declarer's jack, partner discarding the ♣2.

Assuming you win this trick, what is your next play?

BLACK DEUCES (Solution)

North
♠ K J 4
♡ 9 7 4 3
◊ A 6 3
♣ A 8 6

West
♠ 9 8 3
♡ A 10 2
◊ Q 8 7 5 2
♣ Q 3

East
♠ 10 7 5 2
♡ K Q 8 5
◊ —
♣ J 9 7 5 2

South
♠ A Q 6
♡ J 6
◊ K J 10 9 4
♣ K 10 4

The ♡10. If partner's signals are to be trusted, declarer has nine tricks ready to go: three spades, four diamonds, and two clubs.

As partner's strength is in hearts, that is the suit you must attack. But which heart?

You need four heart tricks to defeat this contract, so assume that declarer has a doubleton heart and partner four. You must attack with the ♡10 to *unblock* the suit in case declarer has Jx or Qx, the only relevant doubleton holdings. The rest is up to partner.

KEY LESSON POINTERS

1. IF DECLARER HAS ENOUGH TRICKS IN THREE SUITS TO MAKE HIS CONTRACT, IT DOESN'T REQUIRE A GENIUS I.Q. TO ATTACK THE FOURTH SUIT.
2. WHEN ATTACKING THE "FOURTH" SUIT, ASSIGN PARTNER THE LEAST AMOUNT OF HONOR STRENGTH NECESSARY TO DEFEAT THE CONTRACT AND PLAY ACCORDINGLY.
3. WHEN LEADING FROM A SUIT WHICH CONTAINS ONE HIGH HONOR (A, K OR Q), ONE HIGH INTERMEDIATE CARD (J, 10, 9 OR IN SOME CASES THE 8), PLUS ONE SMALL CARD, CONSIDER ATTACKING WITH THE MIDDLE CARD TO UNBLOCK FOR PARTNER'S GREATER ASSUMED LENGTH.
4. WHEN PARTNER LEADS TOP OF NOTHING VS. NOTRUMP, THIRD HAND SIGNALS ATTITUDE.

(43) ONE JUMP DESERVES ANOTHER

Both sides vulnerable
Dealer West

North
♠ 7 6
♡ 3
◇ J 5 2
♣ A 10 9 7 6 5 4

East (you)
♠ 9 8
♡ 9 5
◇ K 10 9 3
♣ Q J 8 3 2

West	North	East	South
4 ♠	Pass	Pass	6 ♡
All Pass			

Opening lead: ♠K

Declarer wins the ♠A and plays the ♡A K, partner following with the ♡10 and ♡J, dummy discarding a club.

At trick four declarer leads the ◇Q. Partner plays the ◇8.

1. Who has the ♡Q?
2. What is declarer's distribution?
3. Do you take this trick? If so, what do you return? If not, why not?

ONE JUMP DESERVES ANOTHER (Solution)

North
♠ 7 6
♡ 3
◊ J 5 2
♣ A 10 9 7 6 5 4

West
♠ K Q J 10 5 4 3 2
♡ J 10
◊ 8 7
♣ K

East
♠ 9 8
♡ 9 5
◊ K 10 9 3
♣ Q J 8 3 2

South
♠ A
♡ A K Q 8 7 6 4 2
◊ A Q 6 4
♣ —

1. Declarer has the ♡Q. If partner started with ♡QJ10 he would play the ♡Q and then the ♡10 to show you where his sequence starts and where it ends.
2. Declarer is known to hold at least one spade and eight hearts. Judging from partner's play of the ◊8, partner has two diamonds which gives declarer four.
3. Not if you wish to keep your present partner. You would be giving declarer a free entry to dummy to discard his losing diamond on the ♣A. Duck the diamond and take two diamond tricks.

KEY LESSON POINTERS

1. WHEN HOLDING A SEQUENCE IN THE TRUMP SUIT, FIRST PLAY THE HIGHEST AND THEN THE LOWEST TO ALERT PARTNER AS TO YOUR LENGTH AND STRENGTH.
2. PLAYERS WHO COUNT USUALLY KNOW WHAT TO PLAY; PLAYERS WHO DON'T MUST BE GOOD GUESSERS.

(44) FOUR LEVEL TRANSFER

North-South vulnerable
Dealer South

North
♠ 10 3
♡ A Q 8 6 4 3
◇ Q 9 3
♣ 10 4

East (you)
♠ 9 5 4 2
♡ 9 2
◇ 8 5 2
♣ J 6 5 3

South	West	North	East
1 NT	Dbl.*	4 ◇**	Pass
4 ♡	All Pass		

*Penalty
**Transfer to hearts

Opening lead: ♡J

1. Which heart do you play?

   Declarer wins the ♡K and plays a low heart to the queen, partner following with the ♡10. At trick two a low spade is led from dummy.
2. Which spade do you play?
3. Declarer's queen loses to partner's king. Partner returns the ♠6 to declarer's ace. Declarer continues with the ♠J, partner the ♠7, and a club is discarded from dummy. A low diamond is led towards dummy, partner plays the ◇10 and dummy wins the ◇Q. At this point the singleton ♣10 is led from dummy. Do you cover? Why or why not?

FOUR LEVEL TRANSFER (Solution)

North
♠ 10 3
♡ A Q 8 6 4 3
◊ Q 9 3
♣ 10 4

West
♠ K 8 7 6
♡ J 10
◊ A J 10 7
♣ A Q 9

East
♠ 9 5 4 2
♡ 9 2
◊ 8 5 2
♣ J 6 5 3

South
♠ A Q J
♡ K 7 5
◊ K 6 4
♣ K 8 7 2

1. The ♡2. The high-low in the trump suit shows three (or five) trumps.
2. The ♠5. Second high from four small when giving count.
3. Yes. To defeat this contract you must take two diamonds and a club. In order to do this, partner must have the ◊AJ and the ♣AQ. Alas, declarer knows where all the cards are, and if you duck the club, so will he. Partner is now endplayed in three suits. Remember, declarer has a trump entry back to his hand. Your only chance is to cover and hope partner has the ♣9, the biggest card in the deck on this deal. If declarer ducks you can lead a diamond through, and if declarer covers, partner can exit safely with a club.

KEY LESSON POINTERS

1. THE HIGH-LOW IN THE TRUMP SUIT SHOWS AN ODD NUMBER OF TRUMPS. TO HIGH-LOW NEEDLESSLY WITH A DOUBLETON IS A SUIT PREFERENCE PLAY.
2. WHEN GIVING COUNT, PLAY SECOND HIGH FROM FOUR SMALL.
3. WHEN IT GETS DOWN TO THE NITTY-GRITTY, YOU MUST ASK YOURSELF (1) WHERE ARE OUR TRICKS COMING FROM AND (2) WHAT MINIMUM HOLDING PARTNER NEEDS TO DEFEAT THE CONTRACT?
4. A WEAK HAND CAN SOMETIMES PLAY THE ROLE OF THE HERO AND GET THE STRONG HAND OFF AN ENDPLAY BY PLAYING SECOND HAND HIGH.

(45) WEAK JUMP IN COMPETITION

North-South vulnerable
Dealer North

North
♠ A 7
♡ 8 4 2
◇ A K Q 9 5
♣ A Q 7

East (you)
♠ K 6 4
♡ A J 10 7 5
◇ —
♣ 10 6 5 3 2

North	East	South	West
1 ◇	1 ♡	2 ♠*	Pass
3 ♡	Pass	3 NT	All Pass

*Weak (4 –6) with a six card suit

Opening lead: ♣4

1. Dummy plays low, which club do you play?
2. You play low and declarer wins the ♣K. At trick two declarer runs the ♠10. What do you do? Why?
3. You win the trick. What do you return at trick three?

WEAK JUMP IN COMPETITION (Solution)

North
♠ A 7
♡ 8 4 2
◇ A K Q 9 5
♣ A Q 7

West
♠ Q 3
♡ K
◇ J 10 7 6 5 4
♣ J 9 8 4

East
♠ K 6 4
♡ A J 10 7 5
◇ —
♣ 10 6 5 3 2

South
♠ J 10 9 8 5 2
♡ Q 9 6 3
◇ 8 2
♣ K

1. The ♣2. Chances are overwhelming (given the bidding and the dummy) that declarer has either the ♣J or the ♣K. By playing low you avoid blocking the suit and give partner count as well.
2. Take the trick because declarer has no convenient way to return to his hand to run the spades. Count points. Declarer can have no more than six high card points and has already turned up with the ♣K. Consider the spade suit. Partner must have Qx. (If declarer had both honors, or even the queen, he would not have room in his hand for even one heart stopper!)
3. A club. If you return a heart and declarer ducks, you will have created a heart entry to declarer's hand. After he unblocks the ♠A, he will be able to lead a second heart, totally putting an end to the defense.

KEY LESSON POINTERS

1. MAKE SURE YOU KNOW WHAT SYSTEM THEY ARE PLAYING.
2. KEEP TRACK OF DECLARER'S HIGH CARD POINTS AS PROMISED FROM THE BIDDING AND BOTH SHOWN AND INFERRED FROM THE PLAY.
3. ASSUME THAT DECLARER IS PLAYING LOGICALLY—UNLESS HE IS AN OLD PARTNER THAT YOU HAVE GIVEN UP ON.

(46) LONG SUITS

North-South vulnerable
Dealer North

North
♠ 2
♡ A Q 8 7 6 5
◊ 7 5 3 2
♣ K J

West (you)
♠ A K 6
♡ K 10 3
◊ Q 10 8 6
♣ 10 9 8

North	East	South	West
2 ♡*	Pass	4 ♠	All Pass

*Weak

Opening lead: ♣10

Partner tries to cash the ♣AQ but declarer ruffs the second club and plays the ♠Q.

1. What is declarer's most likely distribution?
2. What is your plan?

LONG SUITS (Solution)

North
♠ 2
♡ A Q 8 7 6 5
◊ 7 5 3 2
♣ K J

West
♠ A K 6
♡ K 10 3
◊ Q 10 8 6
♣ 10 9 8

East
♠ 4 3
♡ 4 2
◊ 9 4
♣ A Q 7 6 5 4 3

South
♠ Q J 10 9 8 7 5
♡ J 9
◊ A K J
♣ 2

1. 7–2–3–1. If declarer had four diamonds, partner probably would have shifted to his singleton diamond at trick two.
2. As declarer is marked with both top diamond honors (partner would have overcalled 3♣ holding a top diamond honor to go along with his seven card suit), and the location of the ◊J is in doubt, the sure way of insuring a diamond trick is to kill dummy's heart suit.

   In order to do this safely, you must lead the ♡K. This has the effect of blocking the suit if declarer has ♡Jx. If you lead low, declarer can win the ♡J and later finesse the ♡Q, discarding the ◊J on the ♡A.

   If you don't lead hearts at all, you could wind up getting squeezed in the red suits on the run of the spades. Finally, if you shift to a diamond hoping partner has the ◊J, well, it just isn't there. Sorry.

KEY LESSON POINTERS

1. WHEN A SILENT PARTNER TURNS UP WITH AN UNEXPECTEDLY LONG STRONG SUIT, DO NOT PLAY HIM FOR ANY OUTSIDE ACE OR KING.
2. WHEN PLANNING TO KILL DUMMY'S LENGTH (TO YOUR LEFT) BY LEADING THE SUIT TWICE, CONSIDER LEADING AN HONOR FROM HONOR THIRD IN CASE DECLARER HAS Jx OR Qx.
3. KILLING DUMMY'S LENGTH IS ANOTHER WAY OF AVOIDING A POTENTIAL SQUEEZE.

(47) A WING AND A PRAYER

Both sides vulnerable
Dealer South

North
♠ 7 6 5
♡ K
♢ A K Q J
♣ 10 8 7 5 2

East (you)
♠ Q 8 4 2
♡ 7 5 4 3 2
♢ 10 9 7 3
♣ —

South	**West**	**North**	**East**
1 ♡	2 ♣	2 ♢	Pass
2 ♡	3 ♣	Dbl.	Pass
3 ♡	Pass	4 ♡	All Pass

Opening lead: ♣A

1. What do you play at trick one?
2. You ruff and declarer follows with the ♣K. What do you play now?

A WING AND A PRAYER (Solution)

North
♠ 7 6 5
♡ K
♢ A K Q J
♣ 10 8 7 5 2

West
♠ A J 10
♡ —
♢ 5 4 2
♣ A Q J 9 6 4 3

East
♠ Q 8 4 2
♡ 7 5 4 3 2
♢ 10 9 7 3
♣ —

South
♠ K 9 3
♡ A Q J 10 9 8 6
♢ 8 6
♣ K

1. A heart! Partner must have a seven card club suit to reenter the bidding vulnerable between opponents who have both shown strength. Besides, South would not be too apt to pull a penalty double holding Kx in the trump suit.
2. Once it is conceded that declarer has a singleton club, it becomes imperative to try to cash three spade tricks before some of them vanish on the diamonds. In order to cash three spades, partner must have the ♠AJ10 (with the ♠AK he would have led the suit). If partner has the AJ10 you must lead the queen. Your play works! Bravo, you are the hero.

KEY LESSON POINTERS

1. THE VULNERABILITY, PLUS THE LEVEL AT WHICH YOUR PARTNER BIDS, PLUS THE LOGIC OF THE OPPONENTS' BIDDING FREQUENTLY TIPS OFF THE DISTRIBUTION BEFORE ANYONE ACTUALLY SHOWS OUT.
2. WHEN A CERTAIN NUMBER OF TRICKS ARE NEEDED FROM A PARTICULAR SUIT, ASSUME PARTNER HAS THE MAGIC HOLDING AND PLAY ACCORDINGLY. IF IT MEANS TRUMPING PARTNER'S ACE TO LEAD ANOTHER SUIT THROUGH DECLARER, TRUMP IT. PARTNER WILL UNDERSTAND. . . IF IT'S RIGHT.
3. WHEN DUMMY COMES DOWN AND YOU CAN SEE THAT THERE ARE SIX CARDS MISSING IN A MAJOR SUIT BETWEEN PARTNER AND THE DECLARER, AND BOTH PLAYERS HAVE BEEN BIDDING (BUT NOT THAT SUIT), ASSUME THE SUIT IS DIVIDED 3–3.

(48) OVERRULING PARTNER

Both sides vulnerable
Dealer North

North
♠ K Q J
♡ 9
◇ A 6 3
♣ A K Q 9 4 2

West (you)
♠ 6 4 3
♡ K 8 5
◇ Q 10 7 5 2
♣ 5 3

North	East	South	West
1 ♣	Pass	1 ♡	Pass
3 NT*	Pass	4 ♡	All Pass

*Solid minor, good hand, no interest in hearts

Opening lead: ◇5

Dummy wins the first trick, partner playing the ◇9, declarer the ◇8. The ♣AK are played, declarer discarding the ◇J on the second club. Declarer now leads the ♡9 to partner's ♡A.

1. What distribution do you think declarer has?
   Partner plays the ♣J and declarer ruffs with the ♡J.
2. What do you do now? Why?
   You discard the ◇2 and declarer continues with the ♡10.
3. What do you do now?

OVERRULING PARTNER (Solution)

North
♠ K Q J
♡ 9
♢ A 6 3
♣ A K Q 9 4 2

West
♠ 6 4 3
♡ K 8 5
♢ Q 10 7 5 2
♣ 5 3

East
♠ A 10 7 2
♡ A 4
♢ K 9 4
♣ J 8 7 6

South
♠ 9 8 5
♡ Q J 10 7 6 3 2
♢ J 8
♣ 10

1. Either 2–8–2–1 or 3–7–2–1. You know declarer does not have another diamond loser because he would have discarded it on the ♣Q if he did.
2. No rush to overtrump. By discarding you may be able to promote your ♡8.
3. This time you should win the trick. Even if you catch partner's lone ♡Q, your ♡8 will be high. However, chances are you won't pick off partner's ♡Q. It really doesn't matter. Simply lead a spade to partner's ace and wait for another club play to promote your ♡8.

KEY LESSON POINTERS

1. WHEN DECLARER STOPS DISCARDING LOSERS ON DUMMY'S LONG SUIT, ASSUME HE HAS NO MORE LOSERS IN THE SUIT.
2. WHEN DECLARER STARTS DISCARDING LOSERS ON DUMMY'S LONG SUIT BEFORE DRAWING TRUMPS, ASSUME HE HAS A QUICK TRUMP LOSER OR TWO.
3. BY REFUSING TO OVERRUFF AN HONOR WITH AN HONOR, YOU CAN FREQUENTLY PROMOTE A LOWER SPOT CARD TO A WINNING TRICK.

(49) BLACKWOOD WITH A VOID

Neither side vulnerable
Dealer South

North
♠ K
♡ Q
◊ A J 10 8 7 6
♣ A K J 10 9

East (you)
♠ 6 5 3
♡ A J 5 4 3
◊ K 9
♣ Q 6 5

South	West	North	East
4 ♠	Pass	4 NT	Pass
6 ♣*	Pass	6 ♠	All Pass

*One ace plus a club void

Opening lead: ♡2

You win the ♡A, declarer playing the ♡7.

1. What does partner need to defeat this slam?
2. What do you return at trick two?

BLACKWOOD WITH A VOID (Solution)

North
♠ K
♡ Q
◇ A J 10 8 7 6
♣ A K J 10 9

West
♠ 4 2
♡ K 6 2
◇ Q 5 4
♣ 8 7 4 3 2

East
♠ 6 5 3
♡ A J 5 4 3
◇ K 9
♣ Q 6 5

South
♠ A Q J 10 9 8 7
♡ 10 9 8 7
◇ 3 2
♣ —

1. Partner needs either the ♠Q doubleton or the ◇Q along with the ♡K to defeat this slam.

   If partner has the doubleton ♠Q, return a heart and force dummy to ruff with the ♠K, promoting partner's ♠Q.

   If partner has the ◇Q along with the ♡K, return the ◇K killing the entry to dummy's clubs thus restricting declarer to eleven tricks: seven spades in his hand (if declarer has an eight card suit there is no defense), a heart ruff in dummy, two clubs and one diamond.
2. Partner is more likely to hold the ◇Q than the ♠Q, so shift to the ◇K.

KEY LESSON POINTERS

1. WHEN TWO LINES OF DEFENSE PRESENT THEMSELVES, PLAY FOR THE ONE THAT EITHER REQUIRES THE LEAST, OR, IF THAT'S EQUAL, THE MORE LIKELY HONOR HOLDING IN PARTNER'S HAND.
2. THE LEAD OF THE LOWEST CARD AT A SUIT CONTRACT (PLAYING FOURTH BEST LEADS) SHOWS EITHER A THREE OR A FOUR CARD HOLDING.

(50) ONE JACK

Neither side vulnerable
Dealer North

North
♠ A K J 9
♡ K 10
◊ Q 10 6 4
♣ A 4 2

East (you)
♠ 8 6 4
♡ 6 5 4 3 2
◊ J 9 3
♣ 10 5

North	East	South	West
1 NT	Pass	2 ♣	Pass
2 ♠	Pass	3 ♡	Pass
3 NT	Pass	4 ♣	Pass
4 ♡	Pass	4 NT*	Pass
5 ♣**	Pass	6 ♡	All Pass

*Roman Key Card Blackwood
**0 or 3 Key cards, including the trump king

Opening lead: ◊K

Your agreements are that when a king is led and the dummy has the queen, third hand gives count in the following situations:
(a) Third hand has supported the suit.
(b) Declarer has shown a two-suiter.
(c) Dummy has a long, solid side suit.
(d) The opponents are at the five level or higher.
1. Which diamond do you play at trick one? Why?

ONE JACK (Solution)

	North	
	♠ A K J 9	
	♡ K 10	
	◇ Q 10 6 4	
	♣ A 4 2	
West		**East**
♠ 7 5 2		♠ 8 6 4
♡ 7		♡ 6 5 4 3 2
◇ A K 8 5 2		◇ J 9 3
♣ 9 8 7 6		♣ 10 5
	South	
	♠ Q 10 3	
	♡ A Q J 9 8	
	◇ 7	
	♣ K Q J 3	

1. The ◇J. According to your agreements you should play the ◇3, but you have five trumps. If you can get partner to play a second diamond and declarer also has five trumps, you will promote a long trump for yourself.

   If you play the ◇3, partner may or may not come through with a second diamond play. From his point of view, it could be wrong if, for example, declarer started with:

   ♠Qx ♡AQJxxx ◇x ♣QJ10x

   In any event, you are allowed to give false count if you think it will benefit your side.

KEY LESSON POINTERS

1. YOU AND YOUR FAVORITE PARTNER SHOULD HAVE TRICK ONE SIGNALLING AGREEMENTS.
2. FALSE COUNT SHOULD BE GIVEN ONLY WHEN THIRD HAND CAN STAND A CONTINUATION.

(51) REASONING IT OUT

Neither side vulnerable
Dealer South

North
♠ J 10 7
♡ Q 6 4
♢ K J 5
♣ K J 10 2

West (you)
♠ 5 4
♡ K 10 7 5 3
♢ Q 10 2
♣ A 7 3

South	West	North	East
1 ♠	Pass	2 ♣	Pass
2 ♠	Pass	3 ♠	All Pass

Opening lead: ♢2

Declarer plays the ♢J, partner wins the ♢A and shifts to the ♡9. Declarer plays the ♡J which you win.

1. What do you return? Why?

REASONING IT OUT (Solution)

North
♠ J 10 7
♡ Q 6 4
◊ K J 5
♣ K J 10 2

West
♠ 5 4
♡ K 10 7 5 3
◊ Q 10 2
♣ A 7 3

East
♠ A 3 2
♡ 9 2
◊ A 9 8 4 3
♣ 8 6 4

South
♠ K Q 9 8 5
♡ A J 8
◊ 7 6
♣ Q 9 5

1. The ♡3. Partner should have a doubleton heart, and if he has a trump entry he can put you back in with a club to get a heart ruff. If partner had ♡9xx it is not clear he would have led the ♡9, but even if he did, declarer with ♡AJ and ◊xxx would play the ♡A and ♡J to insure a diamond discard. It can't be right to win the ♡K and shift back to a diamond. In fact, it is rather insulting.

KEY LESSON POINTERS

1. AFTER TRICK ONE VS. A SUIT CONTRACT THERE WILL BE TIMES WHEN A DEFENDER WILL SHIFT TO A HIGH SPOT CARD HOLDING EITHER A DOUBLETON OR THREE SMALL. IT IS ALL BUT IMPOSSIBLE TO LAY DOWN RULES THAT WILL COVER EVERY SITUATION. BUT:
   (1) IF A DEFENDER HAS A DOUBLETON, HE HAS NO OPTION. HE MUST LEAD THE HIGHER CARD IF HE IS LOOKING FOR A RUFF.
   (2) WITH THREE OR FOUR SMALL CARDS THE DEFENDER HAS AN OPTION:
      (a) IF HE WANTS ANOTHER SUIT RETURNED HE SHOULD SHIFT TO A HIGH SPOT CARD AS A LOW CARD SUGGESTS AN HONOR.
      (b) IF HE FEARS ANOTHER SUIT, HE SHOULD SHIFT TO A LOW CARD COAXING A RETURN.
      (c) IF THE BIDDING HAS CLARIFIED EVERYONE'S LENGTH, LEAD HIGH FROM ANY WORTHLESS HOLDING.
      (d) IF COUNT IS THE ONLY ISSUE (CASHOUT SITUATIONS), LEAD HIGH FROM AN EVEN NUMBER OF CARDS, LOW FROM ODD.
      (e) IN CASES WHERE IT IS NOT CLEAR, DECLARER'S PLAY MAY HELP DETERMINE THE POSITION.

(52) NO RUFFING POWER

Both sides vulnerable
Dealer North

North
♠ 8 7 6 2
♡ A K 6
◊ K 7 3
♣ J 6 2

East (you)
♠ 10 4
♡ J 7 5 3 2
◊ 10 8 6
♣ K Q 7

North	East	South	West
Pass	Pass	1 ♠	Pass
3 ♠	Pass	4 ♠	All Pass

Opening lead: ♣10

Dummy plays low and declarer wins. Declarer cashes the ♠AK, partner playing the ♠3 and ♠9, and continues by playing the ♡AK and ruffing a heart in the closed hand. He finally exits with the ♣4 to your ♣Q partner playing the ♣3.

1. What is declarer's distribution?
2. What do you play after winning the ♣Q? Why?
3. You play the ♣K, which holds, partner playing the ♣8. Now what?

NO RUFFING POWER (Solution)

North
♠ 8 7 6 2
♡ A K 6
◊ K 7 3
♣ J 6 2

West
♠ 9 3
♡ Q 10 8
◊ A J 4 2
♣ 10 9 8 3

East
♠ 10 4
♡ J 7 5 3 2
◊ 10 8 6
♣ K Q 7

South
♠ A K Q J 5
♡ 9 4
◊ Q 9 5
♣ A 5 4

1. Declarer must be 5–2–3–3. You can tell from the way your partner played his trumps that he has only two. You know that declarer started with two hearts and you can tell from the lead and subsequent play in the club suit that your partner started with four clubs.
2. You should cash the ♣K so that later you don't get thrown in and forced to lead diamonds. It is bad enough that you have to lead diamonds once; you don't want to have to lead them twice.
3. Declarer is known to have three diamonds. In order to defeat the contract partner must have either the AJxx or the AQxx. If he has either of those two holdings (but no nine), you must attack with the ◊8, surrounding the seven in the dummy! Notice that if you lead this card declarer must lose two tricks. If you lead any other diamond, declarer, if he takes the right view, can avoid the loss of two diamond tricks. (If you lead the ◊6 and declarer plays low from his hand he can hold his diamond losses to one; if you lead the ◊10 declarer can play the ◊Q, again losing but one trick.)

KEY LESSON POINTERS

1. WHEN IT BECOMES APPARENT THAT THE CONTRACT IS GOING TO HINGE AROUND ONE PARTICULAR SUIT, IT IS USUALLY BETTER TO LET THE DECLARER START THE SUIT. IF YOU CAN'T, AT LEAST TRY TO AVOID LEADING THE SUIT TWICE (UNLESS YOU ARE LEADING THROUGH STRENGTH AND THERE IS ABJECT WEAKNESS TO YOUR RIGHT).

(53) CONCEALMENT

Both sides vulnerable
Dealer South

North
♠ Q 10 2
♡ A 10 7 6 5
◇ 6 5 3
♣ 4 3

West (you)
♠ 9 8 5
♡ J 8
◇ K Q 9 4
♣ J 9 6 5

South	West	North	East
2 ♣*	Pass	2 ◇**	Pass
2 NT***	Pass	3 ◇****	Pass
3 ♡	Pass	3 NT	All Pass

*Artificial
**Waiting
***22–24
****Transfer

Opening lead: ♠9

Dummy covers with the ♠10 and partner's ♠J loses to the ♠A. Declarer cashes the ♣AK, partner playing the ♣Q and discarding the ◇2. At trick four declarer leads the ♣10 to your jack, dummy discarding a heart and partner the ♠3.

1. What is declarer's distribution?
2. What do you play now?

CONCEALMENT (Solution)

North
♠ Q 10 2
♡ A 10 7 6 5
◇ 6 5 3
♣ 4 3

West
♠ 9 8 5
♡ J 8
◇ K Q 9 4
♣ J 9 6 5

East
♠ J 7 6 3
♡ K 9 4 3
◇ 10 7 5 2
♣ Q

South
♠ A K 4
♡ Q 2
◇ A J
♣ A K 10 8 7 2

1. 3–2–2–6. Declarer has turned up with six clubs and partner's discard of the ♠3, denying the ♠K, has announced an original holding of four spades (present count) leaving declarer three spades. Therefore, declarer must have doubletons in the other suits to justify a 2NT rebid.
2. The ◇Q! You must establish three diamond tricks before your remaining club stopper is removed. (If not, declarer will take four clubs, three spades and the red aces). Declarer will win and play another club. When you cash the ◇K, leading your honors out of order, partner must unblock the ◇10. A heart shift is futile as declarer is marked with at least one honor to justify his strong rebid.

KEY LESSON POINTERS

1. WHENEVER DECLARER TURNS UP WITH UNEXPECTED LENGTH, HE MAY BE A POINT OR TWO LIGHT FOR HIS BIDDING. THIS IS CALLED COMPENSATION. (TRANSLATION: HE WANTS TO BEAT HIS PARTNER TO THE NOTRUMP AT ANY COST).
2. YOUR FIRST DISCARD IN A SUIT THAT HAS ALREADY BEEN LED IS PRESENT COUNT; IN A SUIT THAT HAS NEVER BEEN PLAYED, IT IS ATTITUDE.
3. WHEN YOU KNOW THE DISTRIBUTION OF TWO SUITS IN DECLARER'S HAND, THE BIDDING OFTEN DISCLOSES THE OTHER TWO.
4. DO NOT LET A DISCOURAGING DISCARD PREVENT YOU FROM SHIFTING TO THAT SUIT IF YOUR HOLDING IN THAT SUIT IS FAVORABLE.
5. WHEN A DEFENDER LEADS EQUAL HONORS OUT OF ORDER AT NOTRUMP, HE IS REQUESTING AN UNBLOCK UNDER THE SECOND HONOR.

(54) MINOR SUIT GAME

North-South vulnerable
Dealer South

North
♠ 10 9 7 2
♡ A K
◇ J 7 6 3 2
♣ A 3

East (you)
♠ A J 5
♡ Q 10 8 7 4
◇ Q 8 5 4
♣ 5

South	**West**	**North**	**East**
4 ♣	Pass	5 ♣	All Pass

Opening lead: ◇K

Declarer ruffs the opening lead and plays the ♣Q and a club to dummy, partner following with the ♣7 and the ♣8.

1. What is declarer's distribution?
2. Declarer leads the ♠10 from dummy at trick four. Which spade do you play? Why?

MINOR SUIT GAME (Solution)

North
♠ 10 9 7 2
♡ A K
◊ J 7 6 3 2
♣ A 3

West
♠ K 8 3
♡ J 9 6 3
◊ A K 10 9
♣ 8 7

East
♠ A J 5
♡ Q 10 8 7 4
◊ Q 8 5 4
♣ 5

South
♠ Q 6 4
♡ 5 2
◊ —
♣ K Q J 10 9 6 4 2

1. 3–2–0–8. If declarer had a losing heart he would have trumped it in the dummy before drawing trumps. Partner's low-high in the trump suit, coupled with a vulnerable vs. not four level opening bid, suggests an eight card club suit. (4–1–0–8 is just barely possible.)
2. The ♠A. To defeat this hand you need three spade tricks. Therefore, partner must have the ♠K. The two critical holdings in the declarer's hand are:

   (a) Qxx (b) Q8x

   With (a) it is correct to play the ♠A, and if declarer later leads the ♠9 (highly unlikely) you must cover with the ♠J. With (b) you must also play the ♠A, but you must duck when the ♠9 is led to give declarer a guess. However, a strong declarer should guess right. If you had ♠AKx, you would have ducked the first time. Having played an honor he should always play you for honor-jack-small. In any case, your best chance is to play the ♠A and hope declarer has not read this book.

KEY LESSON POINTERS

1. WHEN DECLARER HAS A SHORT SUIT IN DUMMY AND DOES NOT RUFF THAT SUIT IN DUMMY, PRESUME THAT DECLARER HAS NO LOSERS IN THAT SUIT. THIS CAN HELP YOU IMMENSELY WHEN YOU THINK YOU HAVE DISCARDING PROBLEMS. IT SHOULD BE SAFE TO DISCARD THAT SUIT.
2. VUL. VS. NOT FOUR LEVEL MINOR SUIT PREEMPTS TEND TO SHOW EIGHT CARD SUITS, ALTHOUGH 7–4 IS ALSO A BALL PARK DISTRIBUTION.

(55) NOT ANOTHER CONVENTION

East-West vulnerable
Dealer South

North
♠ 10 9 3 2
♡ —
◇ 9 8 4
♣ A K Q 9 7 6

West (you)
♠ Q 8 6
♡ A K 9 7 4
◇ K 7
♣ 8 3 2

South	West	North	East
1 NT	Pass	2 ♣	Pass
3 ◇*	Pass	4 ♣	Pass
4 ♠	Pass	6 ◇	All Pass

*Strong five card suit plus 16–17 high card points. Denies a four card major.

Opening lead: ♡K

Dummy ruffs, partner playing the ♡Q. At trick two declarer leads the ◇9, partner the ◇2 and declarer the ◇5.

1. How do you plan to defeat this slam?

NOT ANOTHER CONVENTION (Solution)

North
♠ 10 9 3 2
♡ —
♢ 9 8 4
♣ A K Q 9 7 6

West
♠ Q 8 6
♡ A K 9 7 4
♢ K 7
♣ 8 3 2

East
♠ 7 5 4
♡ Q J 6 3 2
♢ 6 3 2
♣ 10 4

South
♠ A K J
♡ 10 8 5
♢ A Q J 10 5
♣ J 5

As partner can have no more than three high card points (♡QJ), you are going to have to defeat this contract all by your lonesome—but it is going to take courage.

You must duck this trick—quickly! If declarer repeats the diamond finesse you can win the second diamond, and cash whatever hearts you can. It is your only chance.

Declarer doesn't know that your diamond king will fall, and his normal play is to repeat the finesse. Once he does that, there will be no trumps in dummy to protect his heart losers.

KEY LESSON POINTERS

1. THE MOMENT THAT DUMMY COMES DOWN, ADD DECLARER'S AND DUMMY'S HIGH CARD POINTS TO YOUR HIGH CARD POINTS TO DETERMINE PARTNER'S OVERALL STRENGTH.
2. WHEN DUMMY IS VOID IN A SUIT IN WHICH YOU HAVE WINNERS, IT IS OFTEN IMPERATIVE TO TAKE YOUR TRUMP WINNER WHEN DUMMY'S LAST TRUMP IS PLAYED. SOMETIMES THIS MEANS BLANKING A TRUMP HONOR—WITHOUT SHAKING.
3. OF COURSE, IF YOU HAVE THE TRUMP ACE, IT IS MUCH EASIER TO HOLD UP ONCE; BUT CAN YOU DO IT WITH Kx OR Qxx?

(56) INVITATIONAL JUMP

East-West vulnerable
Dealer North

North
♠ Q J 6 5
♡ A 2
◊ J 4 2
♣ A 6 5 4

East (you)
♠ K 10 4 2
♡ J 4 3
◊ A Q 10 8
♣ 3 2

North	East	South	West
1 ♣	Pass	1 ♡	Pass
1 ♠	Pass	3 ♡*	All Pass

*Invitational

Opening lead: ♣J

Declarer wins the ♣KQ, and plays king and a heart to dummy, partner following with a low heart and then the queen. At trick five the ♣A is played from dummy.

1. Do you ruff? Why, or why not?
2. You ruff and declarer discards a spade. What is declarer's most likely distribution?
3. Who do you think has the ♠A and the ◊K?
4. What do you play now?

INVITATIONAL JUMP (Solution)

North
♠ Q J 6 5
♡ A 2
◇ J 4 2
♣ A 6 5 4

West
♠ A 9 8
♡ Q 5
◇ 6 5 3
♣ J 10 9 8 7

East
♠ K 10 4 2
♡ J 4 3
◇ A Q 10 8
♣ 3 2

South
♠ 7 3
♡ K 10 9 8 7 6
◇ K 9 5
♣ K Q

1. You should ruff to prevent declarer from either taking a spade finesse, or, far more likely, leading up to his ◇K.
2. Declarer's most likely distribution is what you see. Another possibility is 1–6–4–2. However, that would give partner a doubleton in the unbid suit, and he might have led it.
3. Partner has the ♠A. If declarer had it, he would be too strong for his bid nor would he be discarding a spade rather than a diamond on the ♣A. If partner has the ♠A, then declarer must have the ◇K to justify his jump rebid.
4. A low spade with a decent partner, the ♠K with the other kind. Your objective is to force declarer to lead diamonds from his hand twice. The only thing that can go wrong with a low spade lead is that partner may win and exit either a spade or a diamond. If he exits a spade, declarer ruffs your ♠K, and exits a low diamond to the jack and queen. Now it is you who are endplayed. Obviously, partner should exit a club. However, if you play the ♠K and then a spade, partner will not get in and won't have a chance to make a mistake.

KEY LESSON POINTERS

1. MOST INVITATIONAL JUMPS AFTER A ONE LEVEL RESPONSE SHOW 9–11 HIGH CARD POINTS. USE THESE FIGURES TO HELP YOU ON DEFENSE.
2. WHEN YOU KNOW A PARTICULAR FINESSE IS GOING TO WORK FOR DECLARER, AND YOU CAN DENY HIM AN ENTRY TO TAKE THAT FINESSE, DO IT.
3. THE CONCEPT OF SAFE EXIT CARDS SHOULD BE PART OF YOUR BRIDGE LORE.

(57) TRUMP ASK

Both sides vulnerable
Dealer South

North
♠ 9 3 2
♡ Q J 8
◇ K 8 6 2
♣ Q 8 7

East (you)
♠ J 10 8 7
♡ A 3 2
◇ A 7 5 3
♣ 6 5

South	West	North	East
1 ♡	Pass	2 ♡	Pass
2 ♠	Pass	2 NT	Pass
3 ♣	Pass	3 ♡	Pass
5 ♡*	Pass	6 ♡**	All Pass

*Are your trumps any good?
**I hope so.

Opening lead: ◇Q

Declarer plays low from dummy and ruffs with the ♡6.

At trick two declarer leads the ♡7 to the ♡Q, partner playing the ♡4.

1. Do you win this trick? If so, what do you return? If not, why not?

   You duck the trick and declarer plays the ♡8 from dummy.

2. Do you win this trick? If so, what do you return? If not, why not?

TRUMP ASK (Solution)

North
♠ 9 3 2
♡ Q J 8
◊ K 8 6 2
♣ Q 8 7

West
♠ 6 4
♡ 5 4
◊ Q J 10 9 4
♣ 9 4 3 2

East
♠ J 10 8 7
♡ A 3 2
◊ A 7 5 3
♣ 6 5

South
♠ A K Q 5
♡ K 10 9 7 6
◊ —
♣ A K J 10

1–2. If partner has a high honor in either black suit, the contract is doomed. Therefore, you must assume declarer has all of the missing high cards. Your only chance to take a second trick is if declarer has four spades and cannot ruff the fourth spade in dummy.

If you win the first heart, declarer will draw one more round of trumps and then test the spades. When he discovers the 4–2 division, he will ruff his fourth spade on the board. The way you can defeat this plan is to duck the first heart, win the second, and return a third. Now declarer must lose a spade trick.

KEY LESSON POINTERS

1. EVEN A BALANCED DUMMY CAN PROVIDE A RUFF FOR DECLARER. IF DECLARER HAS FOUR CARDS AND DUMMY THREE, DECLARER WILL, IF POSSIBLE, LEAVE ONE TRUMP IN DUMMY AND PLAY HIS FOUR CARD SUIT. IF THE DEFENDER WITH THE OUTSTANDING TRUMP ALSO HAS FOUR CARDS IN DECLARER'S SIDE SUIT, THE RUFF CAN BE ACCOMPLISHED.
2. IN ORDER TO THWART DECLARER'S STRATAGEM OF RUFFING A FOURTH ROUND LOSER IN DUMMY, A SHREWD DEFENDER WITH Axx IN THE TRUMP SUIT WILL WIN THE SECOND ROUND OF TRUMPS AND PLAY A THIRD.

(58) IF

Both sides vulnerable
Dealer East

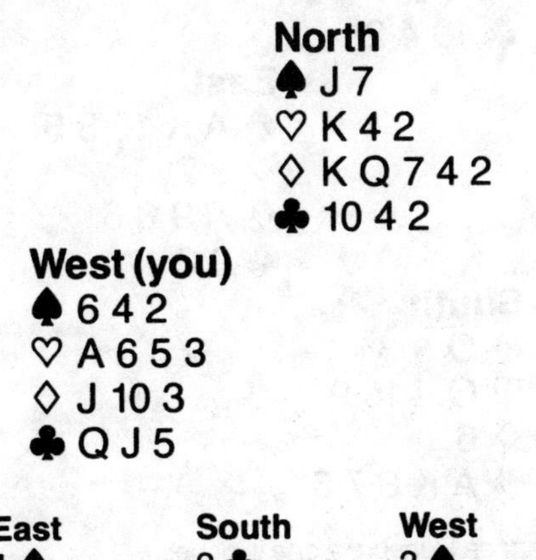

North
♠ J 7
♡ K 4 2
♢ K Q 7 4 2
♣ 10 4 2

West (you)
♠ 6 4 2
♡ A 6 5 3
♢ J 10 3
♣ Q J 5

East	South	West	North
1♠	2♣	2♠	3♣
All Pass			

Opening lead: ♠6

Partner wins the ♠K and shifts to the ♡8. Declarer plays the ♡J.

1. Do you win this trick? If so, what do you return?

IF (Solution)

North
♠ J 7
♡ K 4 2
♢ K Q 7 4 2
♣ 10 4 2

West
♠ 6 4 2
♡ A 6 5 3
♢ J 10 3
♣ Q J 5

East
♠ A K 10 8 5
♡ 8 7
♢ A 9 8 5
♣ 9 3

South
♠ Q 9 3
♡ Q J 10 9
♢ 6
♣ A K 8 7 6

1. Win the trick and return a spade to insure a one trick set.
2. This is what you know: (1) Partner has either a doubleton heart or the Q98. Don't even think about playing partner for a singleton heart. That would give declarer five hearts. Furthermore, with a singleton heart partner would have won the first trick with the ♠A to discourage a spade return. (2) Partner has the ♢A or a club honor to justify an opening bid.

   Putting this information together it is clear that you can defeat the contract two tricks by returning a heart if partner has ♡Q98 plus a minor suit honor. However, if you return a heart, and partner has a doubleton heart along with the ♢A, you have just kissed partner's spade trick goodbye.

   Declarer wins in dummy, cashes two top clubs and then plays two additional rounds of hearts discarding a spade from dummy. A diamond is conceded and your side can only score your trump trick. You have skillfully managed to compress five top tricks into four.

KEY LESSON POINTERS

1. WHEN TRYING TO WORK OUT PARTNER'S HOLDING IN A SUIT AND A NUMBER OF POSSIBILITIES EXIST, GO BACK TO THE BIDDING TO SEE WHICH IS THE MOST LIKELY.
2. WHEN TWO EQUALLY LIKELY POSSIBILITIES EXIST, SELECT THE ONE THAT INSURES A SURE SET RATHER THAN RISK THE CONTRACT FOR AN EXTRA UNDERTRICK.

(59) A LITTLE ROPE

East-West vulnerable
Dealer South

North
♠ J 4
♡ 8 6 3
◇ A Q J 10 8
♣ K 8 6

East (you)
♠ A K 10 7 6 2
♡ A J 5
◇ 7 2
♣ J 9

South	West	North	East
1 ♡	Pass	2 ◇	2 ♠
3 ♡	Pass	4 ♡	All Pass

Opening lead: ♠3

You win the first two spade tricks spearing declarer's ♠Qx.

1. What do you play at trick three? Why?

   You return a third spade which declarer ruffs in dummy, discarding a club from his hand. At trick four a low trump is led from dummy.
2. Which heart do you play? Why?

A LITTLE ROPE (Solution)

North
♠ J 4
♡ 8 6 3
♢ A Q J 10 8
♣ K 8 6

West
♠ 9 5 3
♡ 7
♢ 9 6 4 3
♣ Q 10 4 3 2

East
♠ A K 10 7 6 2
♡ A J 5
♢ 7 2
♣ J 9

South
♠ Q 8
♡ K Q 10 9 4 2
♢ K 5
♣ A 7 5

1 –2. Declarer should have the four missing key cards (♡KQ, ♢K, ♣A) to justify his vulnerable three level free bid. If that is the case the only way to defeat the contract is to give declarer a losing option (a little rope) in the play.

By playing a third spade and then rising with the ♡A and playing a fourth spade, declarer may easily go wrong. If he decides to play for the trump suit to be divided 2 –2, he will ruff high and bang down his remaining heart honor.

KEY LESSON POINTERS

1. WHEN THERE ARE NO MORE TRICKS AVAILABLE IN THE SIDE SUITS, LOOK TO THE TRUMP SUIT.
2. TRUMP PROMOTION PLAYS ARE FREQUENTLY AVAILABLE. THEY INCLUDE: THE "UPPERCUT," RUFFS AND SLUFFS, PROMOTING AN OVERRUFF, MAKING DECLARER FEAR A NON-EXISTENT OVERRUFF (THIS HAND), REFUSING TO OVERRUFF AN HONOR IN ORDER TO PROMOTE A SECONDARY SPOT CARD, ETC.

(60) THIRD SEAT VULNERABLE PREEMPT

Both sides vulnerable
Dealer North

North
♠ K 7 6 3
♡ J 8
◇ 10 7
♣ 9 8 6 5 4

East (you)
♠ Q J 10 8 5
♡ A 10 4
◇ J 8 2
♣ Q 7

North	East	South	West
Pass	Pass	4 ♡	All Pass

Opening lead: ♣K

1. Which club do you play?
   Partner continues with the ♣A which declarer ruffs. At trick three declarer leads the ◇Q to partner's ◇A. Partner shifts to the ♡9. Declarer plays low from dummy.
2. Which heart do you play? What is your plan?
   You duck the heart to declarer's king. Declarer cashes the ♠A, partner playing the ♠2, and exits with a low heart to the jack, partner discarding the ♣2.
3. What is declarer's distribution?
4. What do you return after winning the ♡A?

THIRD SEAT VULNERABLE PREEMPT (Solution)

North
♠ K 7 6 3
♡ J 8
◊ 10 7
♣ 9 8 6 5 4

West
♠ 9 4 2
♡ 9
◊ A 5 4 3
♣ A K J 10 2

East
♠ Q J 10 8 5
♡ A 10 4
◊ J 8 2
♣ Q 7

South
♠ A
♡ K Q 7 6 5 3 2
◊ K Q 9 6
♣ 3

1. The ♣7. Playing the ♣Q under the ♣K shows either a singleton or the ♣J.
2. The ♡4. When you want to prevent a ruff in dummy, you normally clear trumps by playing ace and another. However, in this case you:
   (a) don't mind if declarer ruffs a diamond with the ♡J (it promotes a trump trick for you);
   (b) do not want to give declarer an entry to dummy to finesse your ◊J.
3. 1 –7 –4 –1. You have a perfect count at this point. Declarer has ruffed the second club and partner has shown out on the second round of hearts and has given you a count signal in spades.
4. Exit with the ♡10 and wait for your diamond trick.

KEY LESSON POINTERS

1. THIRD SEAT VULNERABLE PREEMPTS MAY BE MADE WITH STRONG HANDS BECAUSE SLAM IS UNLIKELY AFTER PARTNER HAS PASSED.
2. WHEN YOU HAVE A FINESSABLE HONOR, TRY TO PREVENT DECLARER FROM GETTING TO DUMMY TO TAKE THAT FINESSE.
3. WHEN YOUR INTERMEDIATE TRUMPS SPOTS CAN BE PROMOTED IF DUMMY RUFFS WITH AN HONOR, THERE IS USUALLY NO NEED TO RUSH TO DRAW DUMMY'S TRUMPS. ENTRY CONSIDERATIONS MAY PREVAIL.

(61) THE SPADES HAVE IT

Neither side vulnerable
Dealer East

North
♠ 3
♡ Q J 6 5
♢ Q 10 8 4
♣ A 9 8 7

East (you)
♠ 8 6 2
♡ A 9 4 3
♢ A J 7 2
♣ K J

East	South	West	North
1 ♢	1 ♠	Dbl.*	1 NT
2 ♡	3 ♠	All Pass	

*Negative

Opening lead: ♢K

1. Which diamond do you play at trick one?

   You play the ♢7, declarer plays the ♢6 and partner shifts to the ♡2. Dummy plays low. Which heart do you play?

   Tired of these insulting questions, you win the ♡A, declarer playing the ♡10.
2. What do you play now and why?

THE SPADES HAVE IT (Solution)

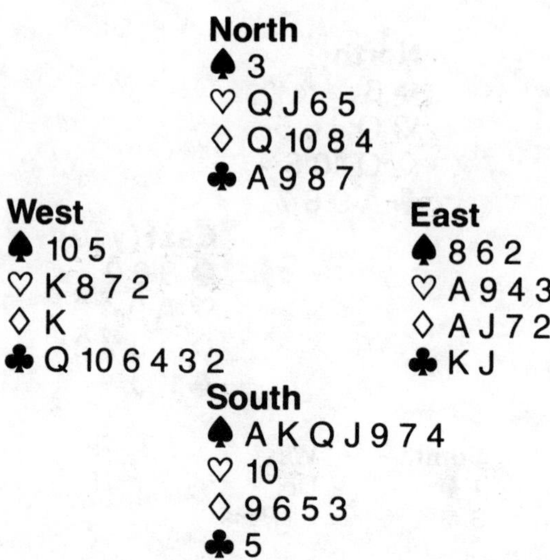

1-2. A low diamond. It seems improbable that partner has another diamond in view of your encouraging signal.

By giving partner a ruff, you still retain control of the suit. Assuming partner makes a normal club shift upon ruffing the diamond, you will come to two more diamond tricks to defeat the contract one trick. Any other play by you allows declarer to make his contract.

KEY LESSON POINTERS

1. WHEN PARTNER LEADS A HIGH HONOR IN YOUR SUIT, RECEIVES A COME ON AND THEN SHIFTS SUITS, ASSUME A SINGLETON.
2. PLAY PARTNER FOR FOUR CARDS IN THE UNBID MAJOR WHEN HE MAKES A NEGATIVE DOUBLE.

(62) WEAK TWOS

North-South vulnerable
Dealer South

North
♠ Q 7
♡ Q 8
◇ Q 9 6 3 2
♣ A K Q J

East (you)
♠ 9 8 4 3 2
♡ A 5 4
◇ J 7 4
♣ 5 4

South	West	North	East
2 ♡	Pass	4 ♡	All Pass

Opening lead: ♣10

1. Dummy wins. Which club do you play?
2. What do you make of the missing spade and diamond honors around the table?
3. At trick two the ♡Q is led. Do you win this trick? If so, what do you return? If not, why not?

WEAK TWOS (Solution)

North
♠ Q 7
♡ Q 8
♢ Q 9 6 3 2
♣ A K Q J

West
♠ A J 10 5
♡ 3 2
♢ A 10 5
♣ 10 9 8 7

East
♠ 9 8 4 3 2
♡ A 5 4
♢ J 7 4
♣ 5 4

South
♠ K 6
♡ K J 10 9 7 6
♢ K 8
♣ 6 3 2

1. The ♣5. Give count, you may wish to try for a club ruff later.
2. Partner does not have the AK of either diamonds or spades (or else he would have led the suit); therefore, declarer has at least one high honor in each suit. Given that declarer has a good suit for his vulnerable weak two, he should have both missing kings and partner both missing aces. If declarer had one side ace and one side king he would have had enough to open 1♡.
3. Play low. Your plan is to win the *second* heart and lock declarer in dummy with a club. Now, whichever side suit declarer plays, partner can win and give you a club ruff. You are hoping declarer started with three or four clubs.

KEY LESSON POINTERS

1. BEFORE PLANNING YOUR DEFENSE, WORK OUT THE POSITION OF THE MISSING SIDE SUIT HONORS FROM THE BIDDING AND THE LEAD.
2. WHEN THERE ARE TWO TRUMPS IN THE DUMMY AND A DEFENDER HOLDING Axx IN THE TRUMP SUIT IS LOOKING FOR A DELAYED RUFF, WINNING THE SECOND TRUMP CUTS COMMUNICATIONS BETWEEN DECLARER AND DUMMY. IT MAY NOT BE POSSIBLE FOR DECLARER TO GET BACK TO HIS HAND TO DRAW THE LAST TRUMP WITHOUT SURRENDERING THE LEAD FOR THE DREADED RUFF. THIS SAME TYPE OF PLAY CAN BE MADE BY A DEFENDER HOLDING Kxx SITTING IN BACK OF THE LONGER TRUMP HOLDING. BY REFUSING THE INITIAL FINESSE AND WINNING THE SECOND ROUND, COMMUNICATIONS BETWEEN THE TWO HANDS CAN BE CUT.

(63) SPLINTER JUMP

Both sides vulnerable
Dealer North

North
♠ K 10 6 4
♡ 2
◊ A K 10 3
♣ 10 8 7 6

East (you)
♠ A Q 9 5
♡ Q 9 4
◊ J 8 7
♣ 9 4 2

North	East	South	West
Pass	Pass	1 ♠	2 ♡
4 ♡*	Pass	4 ♠	All Pass

*Splinter jump, showing a strong hand with a singleton heart plus good spade support.

Opening lead: ♡K

1. Which heart do you play? Why?
   You play the ♡9 and partner continues with the ♡A, dummy ruffing low. Declarer crosses to the ♣A, partner playing the ♣3 and ruffs the ♡10 with dummy's ♠6. Declarer returns to his hand via the ♣K, partner playing the ♣5, and leads a low spade. Partner discards the ♡J.
2. What does that mean?
3. What is declarer's distribution?
4. Declarer inserts the ♠10 from dummy. Do you win this trick? If so, what do you play? If not, why not?

SPLINTER JUMP (Solution)

North
♠ K 10 6 4
♡ 2
♢ A K 10 3
♣ 10 8 7 6

West
♠ —
♡ A K J 8 5 3
♢ Q 9 6 5
♣ J 5 3

East
♠ A Q 9 5
♡ Q 9 4
♢ J 8 7
♣ 9 4 2

South
♠ J 8 7 3 2
♡ 10 7 6
♢ 4 2
♣ A K Q

1. The ♡9 in order to encourage partner to continue hearts. Do you want your partner to shift to a club?
2. Partner is letting you know that declarer has no more hearts. From your point of view, it was possible that declarer had the ♡J.
3. 5–3–2–3. Partner has shown out of spades, helped you out in hearts (not to mention a vulnerable two level overcall), and presumably given you count in clubs. He can't do much more.
4. Your objective is to take three trump tricks. The only way you can lose them is to get couped out of them. To avoid this embarrassment, cash your two spade winners and exit a *diamond* while the clubs are blocked. Now declarer cannot shorten his hand in order to coup you. Had you returned a club, say, declarer wins, enters dummy with a diamond; ruffs a good club; reenters dummy with a diamond and winds up with the ♠J8 over your ♠95. Nor does it help to duck the spade. Declarer cashes his minor suit winners, ruffs a diamond and leads a spade. You wind up taking two, not three, trump tricks.

KEY LESSON POINTERS

1. WHEN DUMMY HAS A SINGLETON, A HIGH SPOT CARD IN RESPONSE TO THE LEAD OF THE KING IS STILL "ATTITUDE" MOST OF THE TIME.
2. IN ORDER TO PROTECT YOUR TRUMP HOLDING IT MAY BE NECESSARY TO REMOVE A DUMMY ENTRY EARLY BEFORE DECLARER CAN BEGIN THE TRUMP SHORTENING PROCESS.

(64) FOLLOW THE PLAY

Both sides vulnerable
Dealer West

North
♠ 10 7 2
♡ K 5
◊ K 9 7 2
♣ A Q 5 2

West (you)
♠ J 9 5 3
♡ A J 10
◊ A J 4
♣ K 6 4

West	North	East	South
1 ♣	Pass	Pass	1 NT*
Pass	2 NT	Pass	3 NT
All Pass			

*12 – 14

Opening lead: ♠3

Dummy plays low, partner contributes the ♠4 and declarer the ♠Q.

1. What is the spade position?
2. How many points do you think partner has?

   Declarer leads a diamond to the king and a diamond to your jack, partner playing the three and the six. You exit with a second spade to declarer's king. Declarer leads the ♣3 to the ♣Q, partner playing the ♣7, and plays a third diamond to his queen and your ace, all following. You continue with the ♠J to declarer's ace, partner following.
3. Declarer now leads a low heart. Which heart do you play? What is your plan?

FOLLOW THE PLAY (Solution)

North
♠ 10 7 2
♡ K 5
♢ K 9 7 2
♣ A Q 5 2

West
♠ J 9 5 3
♡ A J 10
♢ A J 4
♣ K 6 4

East
♠ 8 6 4
♡ 8 7 6 4
♢ 10 6 3
♣ 10 9 7

South
♠ A K Q
♡ Q 9 3 2
♢ Q 8 5
♣ J 8 3

1. Declarer has the AKQ and partner three small. Partner should *not* play third hand high with three small.
2. At most a jack, but probably not. After all, the only jack not visible is the ♣J, and declarer probably has that card for his one notrump bid. Otherwise, he is a very brave man, indeed.
3. The ♡A! You have this hand all locked up. Win your ♡A, cash your spade and exit with a heart to dummy's king. Declarer must now concede a club.

   If you routinely duck the heart, what will you discard on the thirteenth diamond? If you discard a heart, declarer plays a heart. You win, cash your spade and eventually must lead away from the ♣K.

   If you discard your winning spade, declarer can throw you in with a club and end play you in hearts, or throw you in with a heart and end play you in clubs — after cashing the thirteener in diamonds.

   Finally, if you discard a club, declarer can cash the ♣A and drop your king.

KEY LESSON POINTERS

1. THIRD HAND SHOULD NOT PLAY HIGH WITH THREE SMALL CARDS. IT IS MORE HELPFUL TO GIVE COUNT.
2. WORK OUT PARTNER'S POINT COUNT WHEN DUMMY COMES DOWN.
3. VISUALIZE WHAT YOUR HAND WILL LOOK LIKE AFTER MAKING A CRUCIAL DISCARD BEFORE YOU PLAY. VISUALIZE WHAT THEIR HANDS WILL LOOK LIKE IF THEY MUST MAKE A CRUCIAL DISCARD.

(65) THE LEAD OF THE ACE

North-South vulnerable
Dealer East

North
♠ A Q 10 9 7 6
♡ K 5
◊ 9 4
♣ 6 3 2

West (you)
♠ 8 5 3
♡ 4
◊ A K J 10 8
♣ K 10 7 5

East	South	West	North
3 ♡	Pass	Pass	3 ♠
Pass	3 NT	Dbl.	All Pass

Opening lead: ◊A

Partner plays the ◊2 and declarer the ◊7.

1. What is the diamond position?
2. What do you play to trick two? Why?

THE LEAD OF THE ACE (Solution)

North
♠ A Q 10 9 7 6
♡ K 5
◊ 9 4
♣ 6 3 2

West
♠ 8 5 3
♡ 4
◊ A K J 10 8
♣ K 10 7 5

East
♠ 2
♡ Q 10 9 8 7 6 3
◊ 5 3 2
♣ A 9

South
♠ K J 4
♡ A J 2
◊ Q 7 6
♣ Q J 8 4

1. Partner has either three small or a singleton. The lead of the ace demands count if third hand has no honor card (jack or better).
2. A low club. Although it isn't entirely clear which diamond holding partner has, you are far more likely to defeat the contract if he has three small, so assume that he does.

   Once that assumption is made, the club shift follows logically. If partner has the ♠K there is no problem as declarer will not have enough tricks without the spade suit, so there is no need to shift to that suit. Therefore, the choice is between hearts and clubs. A club is better because even if declarer has both the ace and queen, you still haven't given away the contract if partner has the ♡A. However, if you shift to a heart and find declarer with ♡AJx or AQx you won't get a second chance. Declarer will have nine tricks.

   Before the letters come pouring in, yes, the club switch can be tragic if declarer has x AJx Qxx AQJ9xx. In this case anything but a club switch will defeat the contract and a spade switch will massacre it. However, partner is unlikely to open 3♡ with a broken heart suit holding ♠KJx.

KEY LESSON POINTERS

1. THE LEAD OF THE ACE VS. NO TRUMP DEMANDS COUNT IF THIRD HAND HAS NO HONOR (JACK OR BETTER). WITH AN HONOR, THIRD HAND PLAYS IT.
2. WHEN LOOKING FOR AN ENTRY TO PARTNER'S HAND, DO NOT ASSUME IT IS IN DUMMY'S STRONG SUIT. IF IT IS, THAT ENTRY WILL SELDOM RUN AWAY. WHEN DECIDING BETWEEN THE OTHER TWO SUITS, TRY TO GIVE YOURSELF TWO CHANCES—SO THAT IF YOU GUESS WRONG YOU STILL HAVEN'T GIVEN THE HAND AWAY. IN OTHER WORDS, COUNT TRICKS!

(66) LEADING THEIR SUIT

East-West vulnerable
Dealer North

North
♠ K 7 4
♡ Q J 9 8
◊ 10 9 2
♣ A K 6

East (you)
♠ A 9 6 2
♡ 10 5
◊ Q 8 7 4
♣ 9 8 7

North	East	South	West
1 ♣	Pass	1 ♡	Pass
2 ♡	Pass	4 ♡	All Pass

Opening lead: ♣Q

Dummy wins and two rounds of trumps are played, partner playing the ♡6 and ♡7. A second club is cashed and a club ruffed in the closed hand. Declarer cashes the ◊A and exits with a diamond to partner's king. Partner exits with the ◊J!

1. Do you overtake? If you do, what do you return?
2. If you don't, partner's jack holds the trick and he exits with the ♠3. Dummy plays low; which spade do you play?

LEADING THEIR SUIT (Solution)

North
♠ K 7 4
♡ Q J 9 8
◊ 10 9 2
♣ A K 6

West
♠ Q 5 3
♡ 7 6
◊ K J 3
♣ Q J 10 5 4

East
♠ A 9 6 2
♡ 10 5
◊ Q 8 7 4
♣ 9 8 7

South
♠ J 10 8
♡ A K 4 3 2
◊ A 6 5
♣ 3 2

The problem on this hand is: who should attack spades, East or West?

Apparently partner thinks you should attack the suit or else he would not have made that strange play in diamonds. What can partner have in spades to make this play?

If he has the ♠J (he knows you must have the ♠A), he would have to break the suit in case you had the A10(9)x. If partner doesn't have the ♠J, he must have the ♠Q. He has worked out that it is better for you to lead spades unless you have something like the AJ10.

Take a look at the actual combination, the critical case. If partner attacks spades the defense has *no* chance to realize two tricks. However, if you attack by leading a low spade and South makes the normal play of an honor (if he plays the ♠8 he prevails), partner ducks, and you wind up with two spade tricks. To answer the questions:

1. You should overtake and return a low spade for the reasons mentioned above.
2. The ♠9, praying partner has Q8x, the only combination, including the queen, where it doesn't matter who leads the suit first.

KEY LESSON POINTERS

1. WHEN AN EXPERT PARTNER MAKES AN UNUSUAL PLAY, PUT ON YOUR THINKING CAP—SOMETHING IS UP!
2. WHEN YOU HAVE ISOLATED THE PROBLEM (FIRST STEP) AND YOU KNOW HOW MANY TRICKS YOU MUST GET FROM A CERTAIN SUIT (SECOND STEP), YOU MUST ALSO GIVE SOME CONSIDERATION AS TO WHICH DEFENDER SHOULD ATTACK THE SUIT FIRST (FINAL STEP).

(67) STOPPING ON A DIME

East-West vulnerable
Dealer West

North
♠ Q 10 9
♡ 7 6
◊ A K Q 7
♣ K Q J 9

West (you)
♠ J
♡ A Q 10 9 8 4 2
◊ 9 5 4 2
♣ 4

West	**North**	**East**	**South**
3 ♡	Dbl.	Pass	3 ♠
All Pass			

Opening lead: ♣4

Dummy plays the king and partner wins the trick, declarer playing the ♣7. At trick two partner shifts to the ♡5, declarer plays the ♡J and you win with the ♡Q.

1. What do you play to trick three?
   You play the ♡A, partner the ♡3 and declarer the ♡K.
2. What do you play to trick four? Why?

STOPPING ON A DIME (Solution)

North
♠ Q 10 9
♡ 7 6
◊ A K Q 7
♣ K Q J 9

West
♠ J
♡ A Q 10 9 8 4 2
◊ 9 5 4 2
♣ 4

East
♠ A 4 3 2
♡ 5 3
◊ 10 6
♣ A 8 6 5 3

South
♠ K 8 7 6 5
♡ K J
◊ J 8 3
♣ 10 7 2

1-2. A third heart. Partner must have either the ♠K or, more likely, the ♠A. If declarer had those cards along with the ♡KJ, he would have made a stronger response. If partner has the ♠A he will ruff high and give you a club ruff. If not, you still gain when partner has some such trump holding as K765x.

KEY LESSON POINTERS

1. IF PARTNER WINS YOUR SINGLETON LEAD AND RETURNS SOMETHING ELSE,DO NOT PANIC. HE MAY NOT JUST BE GETTING BACK AT YOU FOR ALL THE RUFFS YOU HAVE NOT GIVEN HIM. HE ACTUALLY MAY HAVE SOMETHING IN MIND. HE MIGHT:
(1) BE LOOKING FOR A RUFF OF HIS OWN;
(2) BE IN THE PROCESS OF SETTING UP A DEFENSIVE CROSSRUFF;
(3) HAVE THE ACE OF TRUMP AND FEEL THAT HE CAN GIVE YOU A LATER RUFF;
(4) BE CASHING A HIGH CARD IN ANOTHER SUIT TO SEE YOUR SIGNAL. IF YOU SIGNAL HIGH IT MEANS YOU WANT PARTNER'S SUIT CONTINUED. IF YOU SIGNAL LOW IT MEANS YOU WANT YOUR RUFF, PLEASE.

NOTICE: IF PARTNER GIVES YOU A CLUB RUFF AT TRICK TWO, DECLARER CAN MAKE THE HAND BY DISCARDING A HEART ON A CLUB BEFORE HE DRAWS TRUMPS.

(68) FEATHERWEIGHT OPENING

East-West vulnerable
Dealer West

North
♠ Q 10
♡ Q J 4
◊ A 10 9 4
♣ K 10 6 3

East (you)
♠ A 9
♡ 8 7
◊ K J 3 2
♣ A Q 9 8 7

West	North	East	South
Pass	1 ◊	2 ♣	Dbl.*
3 ♣	Pass	Pass	3 ♡
All Pass			

*Negative (Promising support for the unbid suits)

Opening lead: ♣2

1. Dummy plays low. Which club do you play? Why?
2. Your ♣7 wins the first trick. What is declarer's most likely distribution?
3. Assume you lead a trump. Declarer plays low and partner wins the king and returns the ♡9 to dummy. At trick four the ♠10 is led from dummy. Which spade do you play? Why?

FEATHERWEIGHT OPENING (Solution)

North
♠ Q 10
♡ Q J 4
◇ A 10 9 4
♣ K 10 6 3

West
♠ K 8 7 6 2
♡ K 9
◇ 8 7 5
♣ J 5 2

East
♠ A 9
♡ 8 7
◇ K J 3 2
♣ A Q 9 8 7

South
♠ J 5 4 3
♡ A 10 6 5 3 2
◇ Q 6
♣ 4

1. The ♣7. Partner's lead of a small card after having raised your suit promises the ten or higher in the suit.
2. Declarer might be 5–5–2–1, 4–5–3–1, or most likely 4–6–2–1. With 5–5–2–1 he might have doubled again (takeout) and converted 3◇ to 3♡ showing equal length in the majors. With 4–5–3–1 he might have bid 3◇ over 3♣, having already shown major suit length with the original double.
3. The ♠A. Once partner returns the ♡9 you can assume he has no more hearts (with K 10 9 he would return the ♡10). Therefore, declarer is 4–6–2–1. In order to defeat this contract your partner must have the ♠K. In order to prevent partner from straying off course (if he wins the ♠K and does not return a diamond, you will be endplayed upon winning the ♠A) you should win your ♠A, exit with a spade to partner's king, and sit back and wait for your diamond trick.

KEY LESSON POINTERS

1. WHEN PARTNER LEADS LOW IN A SUIT HE HAS SUPPORTED, HE PROMISES AN HONOR. WITH xxx or xxxx HE SHOULD LEAD HIGH.
2. WHEN HOLDING A DOUBLETON ACE OR KING, CONSIDER RISING WITH YOUR HONOR TO AVOID A POSSIBLE ENDPLAY. IF YOU DON'T GET RID OF THE HONOR, PARTNER MIGHT GET RID OF YOU.

(69) LAID TO REST

Both sides vulnerable
Dealer North

North
♠ Q J 10 5 4 3
♡ A K 2
◇ A 5
♣ 10 6

West (you)
♠ K 8 7 6
♡ 6
◇ J 10 8 7 6
♣ Q 8 4

North	**East**	**South**	**West**
1 ♠	Pass	2 ♡	Pass
4 ♡	Pass	5 ♣	Pass
5 ◇	Dbl.	6 ♡	All Pass

Opening lead: ◇J

Dummy wins, partner signals with the ◇9, and declarer follows with the ◇3. A spade is led to the ace, followed by the ♡Q and a heart to dummy. Partner follows with the ♡5 and the ♡4 as you discard a diamond.

At trick five the ♠Q is led from dummy, declarer discarding the ◇Q.

1. Do you win this trick? If so, what do you return? If not, why not?

LAID TO REST (Solution)

North
♠ Q J 10 5 4 3
♡ A K 2
◊ A 5
♣ 10 6

West
♠ K 8 7 6
♡ 6
◊ J 10 8 7 6
♣ Q 8 4

East
♠ 9 2
♡ 10 5 4
◊ K 9 4 2
♣ K J 3 2

South
♠ A
♡ Q J 9 8 7 3
◊ Q 3
♣ A 9 7 5

1. Crediting partner with three trumps (from his high-low count signal in hearts), it is possible to count declarer's tricks.

   If you win this trick and return a spade, say, killing one discard, declarer will remain with six trump tricks, four spades, plus two minor suit aces for twelve. (Declarer must have the ♣A to have any play.)

   What about ducking this trick? If declarer plays another middle spade, partner ruffs and the spade suit in dummy is dead. Now all partner needs is the ♣K to defeat the contract. The proper play is to allow the ♠Q to hold so that partner can trump the next spade, killing dummy's long suit.

KEY LESSON POINTERS

1. PARTNER'S WILLINGNESS OR FAILURE TO DOUBLE HIGH LEVEL CUE BIDS SHOULD INFLUENCE YOUR CHOICE OF OPENING LEADS.
2. ONE TECHNIQUE OF KILLING A LONG SIDE SUIT IN DUMMY IS TO DELAY TAKING YOUR WINNER UNTIL PARTNER IS VOID. THEN HE TRUMPS THE SUIT ALLOWING YOU TO RETAIN YOUR WINNER.
3. IF THE DEUCE AND TREY OF TRUMPS ARE INTERCHANGED, THIS HAND CANNOT BE DEFEATED! DECLARER CASHES THE ♠A AT TRICK TWO, CROSSES TO THE ♡A AND LEADS THE ♠Q. THE DEFENSE IS HELPLESS BECAUSE THERE IS AN ADDITIONAL DUMMY ENTRY. WORK IT OUT.

(70) WHAT CAN HAPPEN?

North-South vulnerable
Dealer South

North
♠ J 10 8 2
♡ K 9 3
◇ J 5 4
♣ K J 9

East (you)
♠ K 9 7 6 4 3
♡ 10 8
◇ 8
♣ A Q 8 5

South	West	North	East
1 ♡	2 ◇	2 ♡	2 ♠
4 ♡	All Pass		

Opening lead: ◇K

1. Partner continues with the ◇A. What do you discard? Why?
2. You discard a low spade and declarer follows with the ◇Q. Partner continues with the ◇2 which you ruff, declarer following. What do you play now?

WHAT CAN HAPPEN? (Solution)

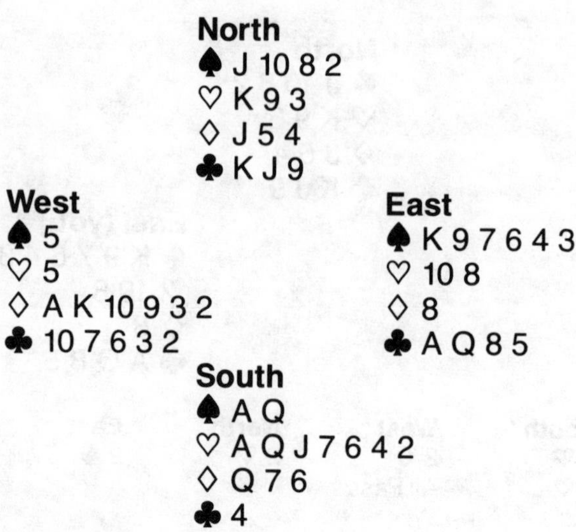

1. You do not want to make a discard that will discourage partner from playing a third diamond.
2. The ♣A. The mice might get at it. Partner cannot have a spade void and return the ◊2 (asking for a club), so he must have a small singleton. If you return a spade and declarer has the hand you see, you will be able to use your ♣A on the next hand. It's gone on this one. Declarer has enough trump entries in dummy to set up a spade for a club discard.

   Yes, if declarer has one more club and one less heart you can defeat the contract two tricks by not playing a club. You can explain all of this to your partner as they are racking up their vulnerable game. He will be very impressed.

KEY LESSON POINTERS

1. DO NOT GET GREEDY ON DEFENSE. IF A ONE TRICK SET IS CERTAIN AND A TWO TRICK SET A 50–50 PROPOSITION, TAKE THE ONE TRICK SET (UNLESS YOU ARE PLAYING TOURNAMENT BRIDGE).
2. WHEN DISCARDING ON PARTNER'S WINNER IN A SUIT WHICH YOU WANT TO RUFF, DO NOT SIGNAL ENCOURAGEMENT IN ANOTHER SUIT. THAT IS WHAT YOU WOULD DO IF YOU WANTED A SHIFT AND DID NOT WANT A RUFF.

(71) THE WAY IT IS

East-West vulnerable
Dealer South

North
♠ 3 2
♡ Q J 10 9
◊ K J 5
♣ A K 10 6

West (you)
♠ A J 9 5 4
♡ A 5
◊ 9 7 6 3 2
♣ 2

South	**West**	**North**	**East**
1 ♣	1 ♠	Dbl.*	Pass
2 ♡	Pass	4 ♡	All Pass

*Negative

Opening lead: ♣2

Dummy wins the ♣K, partner plays the ♣9 and declarer the ♣4. At trick two declarer runs the ♡Q to your ♡A, partner playing the ♡4 and declarer the ♡6.

1. What do you play at this point? Why?

THE WAY IT IS (Solution)

North
♠ 3 2
♡ Q J 10 9
◊ K J 5
♣ A K 10 6

West
♠ A J 9 5 4
♡ A 5
◊ 9 7 6 3 2
♣ 2

East
♠ K 8
♡ 4 3 2
◊ Q 10 8 4
♣ 9 7 5 3

South
♠ Q 10 7 6
♡ K 8 7 6
◊ A
♣ Q J 8 4

1. Either the ace and a spade or a low spade. Partner's spot card is *suit preference* when an obvious singleton has been led. His play of the ♣9 indicates an entry in spades, the higher ranking side suit.

KEY LESSON POINTERS

1. WHEN PARTNER LEADS AN OBVIOUS SINGLETON, THIRD HAND SIGNALS SUIT PREFERENCE. WITH NO PREFERENCE, THIRD HAND PLAYS A MIDDLE CARD AND WATCHES PARTNER SUFFER TRYING TO FIGURE IT OUT.

(72) COURTESY RAISE

North-South vulnerable
Dealer South

North
♠ 3
♡ Q 9 5 3 2
◊ K 7
♣ Q J 10 6 2

East (you)
♠ 7 6 5
♡ A J 8 4
◊ Q J 10 9
♣ 9 3

South	West	North	East
1 ◊	1 ♠	Dbl.*	2 ♠
3 NT	All Pass		

*Negative

Opening lead: ♠J (Denies a higher honor)

1. Which spade do you play at trick one?
   Declarer wins the ♠Q, leads a club to the queen and runs the ♣J to partner's ace.
2. What is the club position?
3. What are declarer's most likely distributions?
4. Partner shifts to the ♡10. The queen is played from dummy. Plan your defense.

COURTESY RAISE (Solution)

	North	
	♠ 3	
	♡ Q 9 5 3 2	
	◇ K 7	
	♣ Q J 10 6 2	
West		**East**
♠ J 10 9 8 4		♠ 7 6 5
♡ K 10 6		♡ A J 8 4
◇ 4 3 2		◇ Q J 10 9
♣ A 7		♣ 9 3
	South	
	♠ A K Q 2	
	♡ 7	
	◇ A 8 6 5	
	♣ K 8 5 4	

1. The ♠5. Signal attitude when partner leads an honor vs. notrump.
2. Declarer must have ♣Kxxx. With ♣Kxx he would have unblocked the ♣K earlier.
3. Either 4–1–4–4 or 3–1–5–4. With 3–2–4–4 declarer would have opened one notrump. (You can tell from the bidding, the lead and the play in clubs that declarer has either 15 or 16 high card points).
4. With the ♡A and return a low heart. Partner is unblocking with K10x for your length. He could see nine tricks for declarer if declarer had the ◇A, so he made a desperation shift to hearts. You, too, can count nine tricks for declarer if he has the ◇A, so you must hope partner has ♡K10x. If partner has ♡10x and the ◇A the hand can no longer be defeated no matter what you do.

KEY LESSON POINTERS

1. WHEN WORKING OUT DECLARER'S POSSIBLE DISTRIBUTIONS, ASSUME WITH A BALANCED HAND PATTERN AND THE RIGHT COUNT HE WILL OPEN ONE NOTRUMP. THEREFORE, WHEN YOU KNOW THAT DECLARER HAS THE PROPER COUNT AND DOES NOT OPEN ONE NOTRUMP, ASSUME HE IS UNBALANCED.
2. HOLDING HONOR-TEN-SMALL, IT MAY BE NECESSARY TO UNBLOCK WITH THE TEN IF PARTNER IS KNOWN TO HAVE GREATER LENGTH. THIS IS PARTICULARLY TRUE WHEN THERE IS A FOUR OR FIVE CARD HOLDING TO YOUR LEFT. CONVERSELY, YOU MUST BE READY FOR SUCH LEADS FROM GOOD PARTNERS.

(73) NO STEALING ALLOWED

North-South vulnerable
Dealer North

North
♠ Q 8 5
♡ 4
◇ A J 10 8 7 5
♣ K J 5

East (you)
♠ K J 7 2
♡ A 3
◇ K Q 6
♣ A Q 7 6

North	East	South	West
1 ◇	Dbl.	4 ♡	Pass
Pass	Dbl.	All Pass	

Opening lead: ♣10

Dummy covers with the ♣J, you win and South plays the ♣4.

1. What do you play at trick two? Why?
2. You play the ◇K which holds, partner playing the ◇3 and declarer the ◇9. What do you play now?

NO STEALING ALLOWED (Solution)

North
♠ Q 8 5
♡ 4
◇ A J 10 8 7 5
♣ K J 5

West
♠ 9 6 4 3
♡ 7 6
◇ 3 2
♣ 10 9 8 3 2

East
♠ K J 7 2
♡ A 3
◇ K Q 6
♣ A Q 7 6

South
♠ A 10
♡ K Q J 10 9 8 5 2
◇ 9 4
♣ 4

1. The ◇K. If you cut declarer's link with dummy, you can save yourself a great deal of later suffering when you will have to discard on the hearts.
2. Another diamond. Partner cannot have three diamonds (he would have played the ◇2) so he must have a doubleton. Declarer will not be able to take a discard on the ◇A—partner will ruff. After this series of plays you must come to a fourth trick in a black suit regardless of declarer's distribution. If you play ace and a trump at tricks three and four, declarer will squeeze you in diamonds and spades.

KEY LESSON POINTERS

1. WHEN YOU HOLD ALL THE MISSING HIGH CARDS AND DECLARER SUSPECTS YOU HOLD THEM, BE WARY OF IMPENDING SQUEEZES.
2. ONE WAY OF AVOIDING A SQUEEZE IS TO KNOCK OUT DUMMY'S ONLY ENTRY BEFORE TRUMPS ARE DRAWN.
3. WHEN PARTNER LEADS A TEN VS. A SUIT CONTRACT AND THE NINE IS NOT VISIBLE, ALLOW FOR A TOP OF A SEQUENCE LEAD. IF THE NINE IS VISIBLE THE LEAD MUST BE FROM SHORTNESS, OR KJ10 IF YOU USE THIS LEAD CONVENTION.

(74) AGGRESSIVE BIDDING

East-West vulnerable
Dealer North

North
♠ Q J 3
♡ A 2
◇ A 9 8 7 3
♣ J 5 3

East (you)
♠ 4
♡ K 8 6 5
◇ K 5 4 2
♣ K Q 9 2

North	East	South	West
1 ◇	Pass	2 ♠	Pass
3 ♠	Pass	4 ♣	Pass
4 ♡	Pass	6 ♠	All Pass

Opening lead: ◇6

Declarer wins in dummy, following with the ◇J from his hand.

1. What do you make of the opening lead?

   Declarer draws three rounds of trumps ending in dummy, partner following with the ♠6, ♠2, and ♠8.
2. What do you discard on the second and third spade?

   Assume you discard a low club and a low heart.
3. At trick five a low diamond is led from dummy. Which diamond do you play? Why?
4. You win the ◇K, and partner discards the ♡J. What does that mean?
5. Now what?

AGGRESSIVE BIDDING (Solution)

North
♠ Q J 3
♡ A 2
♢ A 9 8 7 3
♣ J 5 3

West
♠ 8 6 2
♡ J 10 9 4 3
♢ 6
♣ 8 7 6 4

East
♠ 4
♡ K 8 6 5
♢ K 5 4 2
♣ K Q 9 2

South
♠ A K 10 9 7 5
♡ Q 7
♢ Q J 10
♣ A 10

1. Partner has a singleton diamond. The other possibility, low from Q10x in declarer's first bid suit, is rather far out, to say the least.
2. No need to signal. You have all of the remaining strength. It is partner who should signal for you. The weak hand helps the strong, not vice versa.
3. The ♢K. BY winning the trick you block the suit.
4. It shows the top of a sequence and denies a higher honor.
5. The ♡K. You must attack dummy's entry while the diamonds are blocked. Count tricks. Declarer can score six spades, two diamonds, two hearts and one club. In the end you must get a club or a heart depending upon declarer's distribution.

KEY LESSON POINTERS

1. WHEN PARTNER LEADS DUMMY'S FIRST BID SUIT, HE TENDS TO BE VERY SHORT OR VERY LONG IN THE SUIT.
2. WHEN ONE DEFENDER HOLDS ALL OF THE MISSING HONOR STRENGTH, HE SHOULD NOT SIGNAL. HOWEVER, IT IS IMPORTANT FOR THE WEAKER HAND TO SIGNAL HONESTLY.
3. THE DISCARD OF AN HONOR (JACK OR BETTER) SHOWS THE LOWER TOUCHING HONORS AND DENIES A HIGHER HONOR.
4. WHEN A LONG SUIT IS BLOCKED, ATTACK THE SIDE SUIT ENTRY OF THE HAND THAT HAS THE GREATER LENGTH IN THE BLOCKED SUIT.

(75) SOLID OVERCALL

North-South vulnerable
Dealer North

North
♠ 7 6 5
♡ A 7
◊ Q J 10 9 8
♣ A J 10

East (you)
♠ K 9 8
♡ K Q 10 9 4
◊ A 7
♣ 7 4 3

North	**East**	**South**	**West**
1 ◊	1 ♡	2 NT*	Pass
3 NT	AllPass		

*13–15

Opening lead: ♡3

Dummy plays low. Do you win this trick? If so, what do you return at trick two, if not, why not?

SOLID OVERCALL (Solution)

	North	
	♠ 7 6 5	
	♡ A 7	
	◊ Q J 10 9 8	
	♣ A J 10	
West		**East**
♠ 10 4 3 2		♠ K 9 8
♡ 3 2		♡ K Q 10 9 4
◊ K 3 2		◊ A 7
♣ 8 6 5 2		♣ 7 4 3
	South	
	♠ A Q J	
	♡ J 8 6 5	
	◊ 6 5 4	
	♣ K Q 9	

You should play the ♡9 in order to retain communications with your partner's hand. As declarer has two heart stoppers anyway (you must pay off if declarer started with ♡Jxx), it pays to allow him to take an early trick while your partner retains another card in your suit.

The bidding indicates that your partner can have no more than three high card points. You must hope that those three points are in diamonds and that partner has the ◊K. If so, partner can win the first diamond and clear hearts, leaving you with three established heart tricks along with the ◊A.

If you win the first heart and continue the suit, partner will not be able to return your suit upon gaining the lead with the ◊K.

If you won and switched to a spade playing partner for ♠AJxx or even Q10xx or QJxx (in which case declarer would have to duck two spades and you could then switch back to hearts, you were thinking, but not deeply enough. In fact, you were dreaming.

With three high card points, partner can hardly hold ♠AJxx. Furthermore, if declarer has only one spade stopper (which means declarer has the ◊K), he would have grabbed the opening lead (to prevent a spade switch), and knocked out the ◊A.

KEY LESSON POINTERS

1. WHEN DECLARER IS KNOWN TO HOLD TWO STOPPERS IN THE SUIT THE DEFENSE WISHES TO ESTABLISH, IT IS USUALLY RIGHT TO ALLOW THE DECLARER TO WIN AN EARLY TRICK IN ORDER TO RETAIN COMMUNICATIONS.
2. WHEN CONSIDERING A DEFENSIVE PLAY WHERE PARTNER NEEDS A PARTICULAR HOLDING, ASK YOURSELF IF PARTNER CAN REASONABLY HOLD WHAT YOU WANT HIM TO HOLD, OR ARE YOU DREAMING AGAIN? ALSO ASK YOURSELF IF DECLARER WOULD HAVE PLAYED THE HAND THE WAY HE IS PLAYING IT, IF PARTNER HAS WHAT YOU WANT HIM TO HAVE. THIS IS NOT A GAME FOR LAZY PLAYERS.

(76) WAKE UP CALL

East-West vulnerable
Dealer South

North
♠ A 3 2
♡ A Q 5
◇ J 10 6
♣ K Q J 9

West (you)
♠ J 7
♡ 9 5 4 3 2
◇ A K Q 5 4
♣ 10

South	West	North	East
3 ♠	Pass	4 ♠	All Pass

Opening lead: ◇Q (Q from AKQ)

Partner plays the ◇9 and declarer the ◇2.

1. What is the diamond position?
2. What do you play now?

   You continue with the ◇A, showing an odd number of diamonds, and partner plays the ◇7 and declarer the ◇3.
3. What do you play to trick three?

   You continue with the ◇K, partner discarding the ♣A (you've read right), and declarer following.
4. What is going on, and what do you play to trick four?

WAKE UP CALL (Solution)

North
♠ A 3 2
♡ A Q 5
◊ J 10 6
♣ K Q J 9

West
♠ J 7
♡ 9 5 4 3 2
◊ A K Q 5 4
♣ 10

East
♠ K
♡ 8 7
◊ 9 7
♣ A 8 7 6 5 4 3 2

South
♠ Q 10 9 8 6 5 4
♡ K J 10
◊ 8 3 2
♣ —

1. Partner has a singleton or a doubleton. With four cards, partner plays second highest.

2–4. A fourth diamond. Partner didn't discard the ♣A to get you to lead a heart, he had other ways of doing that. Having set up all of those clubs in dummy, partner was simply trying to tell you to lead a fourth diamond in order to promote his singleton king of spades. He knew your third diamond was going to cash.

KEY LESSON POINTERS

1. IF YOU ADOPT THE LEAD OF THE QUEEN FROM ACE-KING-QUEEN, THIRD HAND GIVES COUNT. THE OPENING LEADER CAN GIVE COUNT TOO. WITH AN ORIGINAL HOLDING OF AN ODD NUMBER OF CARDS, HE CONTINUES WITH THE ACE; WITH AN ORIGINAL HOLDING OF AN EVEN NUMBER OF CARDS, HE CONTINUES WITH THE KING.
2. WHEN PARTNER MAKES A TERRIFYING DISCARD, WAKE UP! HE WANTS AN UNUSUAL PLAY, USUALLY A TRUMP PROMOTION PLAY OF ONE SORT OR ANOTHER.

(77) WITH THIS HAND?

Neither side vulnerable
Dealer North

North
♠ Q 9 4
♡ 10 9
◇ A Q 5 4
♣ A Q 10 4

East (you)
♠ K 8 5 2
♡ J 7 3 2
◇ 6 3
♣ 9 8 7

North	East	South	West
1 ◇	Pass	1 ♠	Pass
2 ♠	Pass	2 NT	Pass
3 NT	All Pass		

Opening lead: ◇J

1. Dummy plays low, which diamond do you play?
2. How many points do you expect declarer to have?
3. How many spades?
   Declarer wins the ◇K and leads a low spade to partner's ace. Partner exits with the ◇10 taken in dummy, declarer following. The ♠Q goes to your king, partner discarding a low club.
4. What do you play now?

WITH THIS HAND? (Solution)

North
♠ Q 9 4
♡ 10 9
◇ A Q 5 4
♣ A Q 10 4

West
♠ A
♡ A Q 8 5
◇ J 10 9 8 7
♣ 6 5 3

East
♠ K 8 5 2
♡ J 7 3 2
◇ 6 3
♣ 9 8 7

South
♠ J 10 7 6 3
♡ K 6 4
◇ K 2
♣ K J 2

1. The ◇6. Partner will know soon enough that you don't have an honor. When you are known *not* to have an honor, signal count.
2. Between 10–12 high card points.
3. In theory, four. Yes, South has turned up with five spades, but his bidding indicated four. Some people just can't be trusted.
4. It's about time to play hearts, don't you think? The catch is to play the right heart. You need at least three *quick* heart tricks to defeat this contract since declarer is known to have three spade tricks, three diamond tricks and a likely four club tricks in plain view.

   In order to get at least three heart tricks, partner must have the ♡AQ8(x). If partner has that holding you must counter with the ♡J to prevent declarer from ducking a lower heart lead around to dummy's ♡109. Your clever defense defeats the contract two tricks.

KEY LESSON POINTERS

1. DECLARER MAY NOT HAVE THE DISTRIBUTION (OR THE POINT COUNT) THAT HIS BIDDING INDICATES, NEVERTHELESS, TRY TO USE THE BIDDING TO FORM A PICTURE OF DECLARER'S HAND.
2. WHEN A DEFENDER CANNOT AFFORD TO ALLOW DECLARER TO DUCK HIS LEAD AROUND TO DUMMY, HE MUST FORCE THE PLAY BY ATTACKING WITH AN HONOR CARD, EVEN WHEN LACKING A LOWER TOUCHING HONOR.

(78) AGREEMENTS

Neither side vulnerable
Dealer East

North
♠ K 10 8
♡ J 4
◊ K Q J 7 6
♣ 7 5 2

East (you)
♠ A J
♡ Q 9 5
◊ 4 2
♣ A K 10 9 4 3

East	South	West	North
1 ♣	1 ♡	1 ♠	2 ◊
3 ♣	4 ◊	Pass	4 ♡
All Pass			

Opening lead: ♣Q

1. Which club do you play at trick one? Why?
2. You play the ♣10 and partner switches to the ♠4. Dummy plays low. Which spade do you play? Why?

AGREEMENTS (Solution)

West	North	East
	North ♠ K 10 8 ♡ J 4 ◇ K Q J 7 6 ♣ 7 5 2	
West ♠ Q 7 5 4 3 2 ♡ 10 6 ◇ 8 3 ♣ Q J 8		**East** ♠ A J ♡ Q 9 5 ◇ 4 2 ♣ A K 10 9 4 3
	South ♠ 9 6 ♡ A K 8 7 3 2 ◇ A 10 9 5 ♣ 6	

1. ♣10, asking for a spade shift.
2. ♠J.

KEY LESSON POINTERS

1. WHEN YOU HAVE SHOWN A SIX CARD SUIT OR LONGER AND YOUR PARTNER LEADS THE ACE, KING, OR QUEEN, THE FOLLOWING AGREEMENTS ARE USEFUL:
   (a) UNDER THE ACE: THE KING SHOWS SOLIDITY (NOT SUIT PREFERENCE); THE QUEEN, JACK, AND TEN ARE SUIT PREFERENCE; THE LOWEST SPOT POSSIBLE IS ALSO SUIT PREFERENCE;
   (b) UNDER THE KING: THE QUEEN SHOWS THE JACK; THE JACK AND TEN ARE SUIT PREFERENCE; THE LOWEST SPOT IS SUIT PREFERENCE;
   (c) UNDER THE QUEEN: THE JACK AND TEN ARE SUIT PREFERENCE; THE LOWEST SPOT IS SUIT PREFERENCE.

   NOTICE THAT HIGH SPOT CARDS (TYPICALLY AN 8 OR A 9) HAVE NOT BEEN DISCUSSED. IF PARTNER PLAYS A HIGH SPOT CARD, AND YOU CAN TELL FROM THE BIDDING THAT HE MUST HAVE MORE THAN TWO LOWER SPOT CARDS, THE SPOT CARD IS SUIT PREFERENCE. FOR EXAMPLE:

West	North	East
	North (dummy) ♠ Q J 10 7	
West ♠ A		**East** ♠ 9
	South ♠ 2	

   HEARTS ARE TRUMPS AND WEST LEADS THE ♠A. (EAST'S 6 CARD SUIT). EAST'S PLAY OF THE ♠9 IS A SUIT PREFERENCE PLAY FOR DIAMONDS AS HE MUST HAVE MORE THAN TWO SPOT CARDS LOWER THAN THE NINE.
2. IN A CASHOUT SITUATION, WHEN ONE DEFENDER IS LEADING THROUGH A KING, THE LEAD OF A LOW CARD PROMISES THE QUEEN (OR ACE). OTHERWISE, A HIGH SPOT CARD SHOULD BE LED—NOT FOURTH BEST.

   Notice: With a club continuation, South ruffs and plays three rounds of trumps. Now the defense gets only one spade trick.

(79) MORE AGREEMENTS

Both sides vulnerable
Dealer South

North
♠ 7
♡ J 10 6 5 4
◊ K Q 10 8 7 2
♣ 10

West (you)
♠ K J 6 5 2
♡ 7
◊ A 4 3
♣ A 6 5 3

South	West	North	East
1 ♡	1 ♠	4 ♡	4 ♠
5 ♡	Dbl.	All Pass	

Opening lead: ♣A

1. Partner plays the ♣2, what do you play at trick two?
2. Partner plays the ♣Q, what do you play at trick two?

MORE AGREEMENTS (Solution)

North
♠ 7
♡ J 10 6 5 4
♢ K Q 10 8 7 2
♣ 10

West
♠ K J 6 5 2
♡ 7
♢ A 4 3
♣ A 6 5 3

East
♠ A Q 4
♡ 8
♢ J 9 6
♣ Q J 9 7 4 2

South
♠ 10 9 8 3
♡ A K Q 9 3 2
♢ 5
♣ K 8

1. The ♢A followed by another ♢.
2. The ♠5.

KEY LESSON POINTERS

1. WHEN AN ACE OR KING IS LED IN AN UNBID SUIT OF WHICH DUMMY HAS A SINGLETON PLUS A STRONG SIDE SUIT, PLUS GOOD TRUMPS, PARTNER'S CARD IS SUIT PREFERENCE.
2. THERE IS ONLY ONE TRAP IN THE ABOVE LESSON POINTER. SOMETIMES IT IS RIGHT TO FORCE DUMMY TO TRUMP. WHEN THAT POSSIBILITY EXISTS, A RELATIVELY HIGH SPOT CARD, RATHER THAN AN HONOR, SHOULD BE PLAYED TO ASK FOR A CONTINUATION (SEE HAND 63).

(80) LOOKING FOR FOUR

Both sides vulnerable
Dealer South

North
♠ Q 10 4
♡ A 2
◇ K 8 4 3
♣ K J 10 3

East (you)
♠ A 9
♡ 5 4 3
◇ A 7 6 5 2
♣ 9 7 4

South	West	North	East
1 ♡	Pass	2 NT	Pass
3 ♣	Pass	4 ♣	Pass
4 ♡	All Pass		

Opening lead: ♠3

1. What is declarer's distribution? (All four suits!)
2. Dummy plays low, which spade do you play?
3. You win the ♠A, declarer following with the ♠7. What do you play to trick two?

LOOKING FOR FOUR (Solution)

North
♠ Q 10 4
♡ A 2
♢ K 8 4 3
♣ K J 10 3

West
♠ K 6 5 3 2
♡ 10 9 6
♢ Q 10 9
♣ 8 2

East
♠ A 9
♡ 5 4 3
♢ A 7 6 5 2
♣ 9 7 4

South
♠ J 8 7
♡ K Q J 8 7
♢ J
♣ A Q 6 5

1. Declarer must be 3–5–1–4. Even though you can't see the ♠2, you know partner has it. If declarer had it, declarer would have four spades plus a diamond void. If declarer were void in diamonds, partner would have led a diamond holding QJ109.
2. The ♠A. If you played the ♠9, or even thought about it, don't tell a soul.
3. The ♢A. The idea is to make life easy, not miserable, for partner. If you return the ♠9 and declarer plays the ♠J, a card he is known to hold, partner is not going to be sure who has the missing spade. If he mistakenly thinks you have it, he will shift to a diamond hoping for two tricks in the suit. From partner's point of view, declarer may be 2–5–2–4. If so, a diamond switch is necessary before a diamond is discarded on the ♠Q. After cashing your ♢A, return your spade. Now partner can have no further problem. You have taken care of him . . . again.

KEY LESSON POINTERS

1. WHEN DECLARER CAN HAVE ONE OF TWO POSSIBLE HAND PATTERNS, ASK YOURSELF IF PARTNER'S OPENING LEAD IS LOGICAL GIVEN THE HAND PATTERN YOU ARE ASSUMING. FOR EXAMPLE, HERE YOU CAN ELIMINATE HAND PATTERNS WITH DIAMOND VOIDS BECAUSE PARTNER WOULD HAVE LED DIFFERENTLY.
2. WHEN TRYING FOR A RUFF, PARTNER MAY NOT KNOW YOU ARE VOIDING YOURSELF IN A SUIT, PARTICULARLY IF THE SPOTS ARE AMBIGUOUS OR DIFFICULT TO READ. IF YOU CAN BUILD A FENCE AROUND PARTNER BY FIRST CASHING AN ACE IN A SUIT PARTNER MAY BE TEMPTED TO LEAD, CASH IT. IN OTHER WORDS, REDUCE YOUR PARTNER'S LOSING OPTIONS. HE'LL LOVE YOU FOREVER.

(81) PUSH, PUSH, PUSH

North-South vulnerable
Dealer South

North
♠ 10 8 5 3
♡ 10 6 3
◇ A K 8 2
♣ 7 4

East (you)
♠ 7 6
♡ Q 8 5 4
◇ 10 9
♣ J 9 6 3 2

South	West	North	East
1 ♠	1 NT	2 ♠	Pass
Pass	2 NT	3 ♠	All Pass

Opening lead: ♣K

Declarer wins, crosses to the ◇A and runs the ♠8 to partner's ♠Q. Partner exits with the ◇Q to dummy's ◇K. A club is ruffed in the closed hand and the ♠K goes to partner's ace. Partner cashes the ◇J and exits with the ♡2. Dummy plays low.

1. What is declarer's distribution?
2. Which heart do you play? Why?

PUSH, PUSH, PUSH (Solution)

North
♠ 10 8 5 3
♡ 10 6 3
◊ A K 8 2
♣ 7 4

West
♠ A Q
♡ A 9 2
◊ Q J 5
♣ K Q 10 8 5

East
♠ 7 6
♡ Q 8 5 4
◊ 10 9
♣ J 9 6 3 2

South
♠ K J 9 4 2
♡ K J 7
◊ 7 6 4 3
♣ A

1. Declarer must be 5–3–4–1. Partner would not have played the ◊Q at trick four holding ◊QJxx; he would have exited with a low diamond after seeing your ◊10.
2. The ♡8. You need two heart tricks to defeat this contract and partner's possible heart holdings are: (a) Kxx, (b) Axx, (c) KJx, (d) A9x, (e) AJx.

   If partner has (a), (b), or (e), it doesn't matter which heart you play. If partner has (a) or (b), you are entitled to one heart trick. If partner has (e), you can't get out of your own way. You always get two. Therefore, concentrate on (c) and (d).

   If partner has (c) you must play the queen, but if partner has (d) you must play the ♡8. How can you tell? The clue is that a good partner would not lead low holding (c). He would anticipate your problem and lead an honor. When he does not, he must have (d) and, therefore, you must play the ♡8.

KEY LESSON POINTERS

1. WHEN TRYING TO WORK OUT THE BEST PLAY IN A CRITICAL SUIT, YOU MUST (1) KNOW HOW MANY TRICKS YOU NEED IN THE SUIT; (2) SAVE WEAR AND TEAR ON YOUR FRAGILE BRAIN BY NOT WORRYING ABOUT IRRELEVANT COMBINATIONS; (3) ASSUME PARTNER IS LEADING THE PROPER CARD IN THE SUIT—GRANTED, A DANGEROUS ASSUMPTION IN SOME CASES.

(82) SEE IT?

East-West vulnerable
Dealer South

North
♠ K Q 9 8 7 6
♡ J 9 2
◇ A
♣ J 10 4

West (you)
♠ A J 3
♡ 10 8 6
◇ K Q 10 5
♣ 8 7 2

South	**West**	**North**	**East**
1 ♡	Pass	1 ♠	Pass
2 ♣	Pass	3 ♡	Pass
4 ♣	Pass	4 ◇	Pass
4 NT	Pass	5 ◇	Pass
6 ♡	All Pass		

Opening lead: ◇K

Partner plays the ◇2 and declarer the ◇4. Declarer crosses to the ♡A, partner playing the ♡4, and leads the ♠2.

1. Which spade do you play? Why?
2. Assume you win the ♠A and partner plays the ♠4. What now?

SEE IT? (Solution)

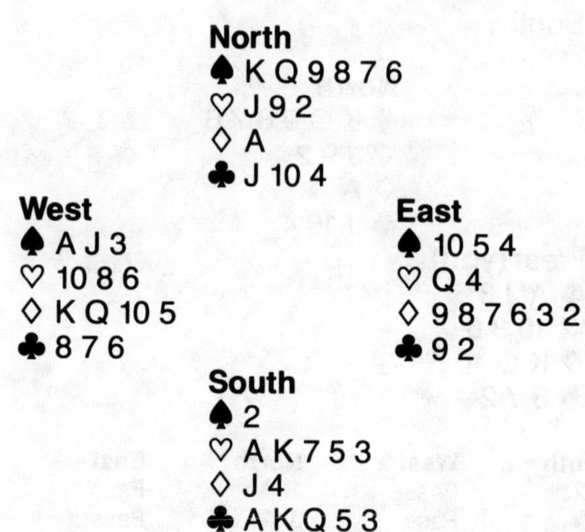

1. There is no good reason for ducking the spade, and there is an excellent chance that declarer has a singleton. (Keep in mind that if declarer needs anything in clubs, it's there.)
2. Your only chance is to hope partner has ♡Qx and play the ♢Q, forcing dummy. This will promote your ♡10 to the setting trick.

   Next time North-South hold these cards, they should arrange to play the hand in 6♣, a contract that can be made if the ♡Q is doubleton.

KEY LESSON POINTERS

1. WHEN SIDE SUIT TRICKS ARE NOT FORTHCOMING, LOOK TO THE TRUMP SUIT.
2. FORCING THE DUMMY TO TRUMP IS ONE WAY OF PROMOTING SECONDARY HONORS IN THE TRUMP SUIT. GIVING A RUFF AND A SLUFF IS ANOTHER.

(83) THE HEARTS HAVE IT

Neither side vulnerable
Dealer North

North
♠ A K Q 9 6 2
♡ 9
♢ J 10 8 7 4
♣ 9

East (you)
♠ 10 7 5 3
♡ J 5 3
♢ A 9 5
♣ 10 3 2

North	East	South	West
1 ♠	Pass	3 ♡	Pass
3 ♠	Pass	4 ♣	Pass
4 ♠	Pass	6 ♡	All Pass

Opening lead: ♢3

Dummy plays low; you win the ace, and declarer plays the ♢2.

1. How do you read the diamond position?
2. What do you return at trick two?

THE HEARTS HAVE IT (Solution)

North
♠ A K Q 9 6 2
♡ 9
◊ J 10 8 7 4
♣ 9

West
♠ J 8 4
♡ 7 6
◊ Q 6 3
♣ Q 8 7 6 4

East
♠ 10 7 5 3
♡ J 5 3
◊ A 9 5
♣ 10 3 2

South
♠ —
♡ A K Q 10 8 4 2
◊ K 2
♣ A K J 5

1. Partner can't have the ◊KQ, and declarer wouldn't leap to a slam without a control in the unbid suit. Therefore, declarer has ◊K2.
2. The ♡J. Lacking the ◊A, South should have at least seven solid hearts for his leap. Also, his failure to Blackwood suggests a void. Clearly the best return is a trump. However, you must be careful to lead the ♡J, lest declarer, in his desperation to get to dummy, plays low if you lead a low trump. Now wouldn't that be something? Your trump return nets you an additional two club tricks.

KEY LESSON POINTERS

1. WHEN A GOOD PLAYER LEAPS TO SLAM WITHOUT USING SOME FORM OF BLACKWOOD, HE EITHER HAS: (1) FIRST OR SECOND ROUND CONTROL IN ANY UNBID SUIT, (2) A VOID.
2. WHEN DEFENDING AGAINST AN ENTRYLESS DUMMY, BE SURE IT REMAINS ENTRYLESS. DO NOT ALLOW DECLARER TO GET OVER THERE WITH A SEEMINGLY INNOCENT LOOKING SPOT CARD.

(84) AND NOW?

East-West vulnerable
Dealer West

North
♠ Q J 10
♡ K 10
♢ 7 5 3
♣ A K Q 10 4

West (you)
♠ A 3 2
♡ J 9 8 7 6
♢ A K 6 4
♣ J

West	North	East	South
1 ♡	1 NT	Pass	3 ♠*
Pass	4 ♠	All Pass	

*Forcing

Opening lead: ♢K

Partner plays the ♢2 and declarer the ♢8.

1. What do you play at trick two? Why?

AND NOW? (Solution)

North
♠ Q J 10
♡ K 10
◇ 7 5 3
♣ A K Q 10 4

West
♠ A 3 2
♡ J 9 8 7 6
◇ A K 6 4
♣ J

East
♠ 6 5
♡ 4 3 2
◇ Q 2
♣ 9 8 6 5 3 2

South
♠ K 9 8 7 4
♡ A Q 5
◇ J 10 9 8
♣ 7

1. The ◇A. When you stop to think about it, you have two chances to defeat this contract. Both of them will work if you cash the ◇A.
   (1) Partner has a singleton diamond or Q2. If you don't cash the ◇A declarer can discard a diamond from dummy on the third heart, draw trumps and make the contract easily.
   (2) Partner has a singleton heart along with two spades. If nothing exciting happens when you cash the ◇A, shift to a heart. If partner has a singleton you can give him a ruff upon winning the first trump lead.

KEY LESSON POINTERS

1. WHEN THIRD HAND HAS Qx AND PARTNER LEADS THE KING VS. A SUIT CONTRACT, PLAY LOW UNLESS THE JACK IS IN THE DUMMY. THE PLAY OF THE QUEEN UNDER THE KING PROMISES EITHER THE JACK OR A SINGLETON. PARTNER MAY UNDERLEAD TO YOUR PRESUMED JACK AND HEAVEN HELP THE PLAYER WHO PRODUCES A SMALL CARD WHEN THIS HAPPENS!
2. EVEN THOUGH THE LOWEST SPOT CARD IN RESPONSE TO THE KING IS A DISCOURAGING SIGNAL, THE OPENING LEADER MUST ALLOW FOR THE POSSIBILITY OF A DOUBLETON QUEEN OR A SINGLETON.

(85) FLIP SIDE

North-South vulnerable
Dealer South

North
♠ Q J 8 4
♡ —
♢ 7 5 4 3 2
♣ A K Q 9

West (you)
♠ K 9 7 2
♡ 8 6 2
♢ J
♣ J 10 8 7 6

South	West	North	East
4 ♡	All Pass		

Opening lead: ♢J

Partner wins the ♢A, declarer playing the ♢K, and continues with the ♠A. Which spade do you play? Why?

FLIP SIDE (Solution)

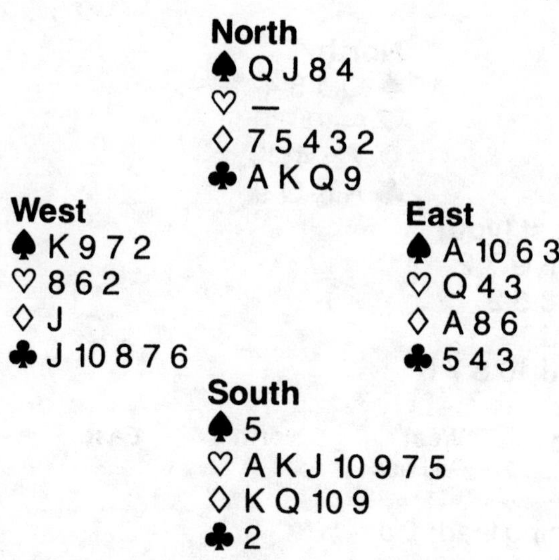
North
♠ Q J 8 4
♡ —
◊ 7 5 4 3 2
♣ A K Q 9

West
♠ K 9 7 2
♡ 8 6 2
◊ J
♣ J 10 8 7 6

East
♠ A 10 6 3
♡ Q 4 3
◊ A 8 6
♣ 5 4 3

South
♠ 5
♡ A K J 10 9 7 5
◊ K Q 10 9
♣ 2

1. The ♠2. You want to ruff a diamond, don't you, or have you forgotten that you are now void in the suit?

Of course, it is possible that declarer has a singleton diamond and that partner has a doubleton ace of spades, in which case a spade continuation is best; however, it is more likely that partner fears the club suit and doesn't know which way to go — diamond ruff or cash two spade tricks.

KEY LESSON POINTERS

1. IF YOU LEAD A SINGLETON, AND SEE PARTNER WIN THE ACE AND PLAY A WINNER IN ANOTHER SUIT, DON'T DESPAIR. PLAY LOW AND GET YOUR RUFF ON THE NEXT TRICK. PARTNER KNOWS WHAT HE IS DOING. REMEMBER, PARTNER DOESN'T ALWAYS KNOW WHETHER OR NOT YOU HAVE LED A SINGLETON. YOUR SIGNAL AT TRICK TWO WILL INFORM HIM — YOUR SIGNAL, NOT THE "LOOK" ON YOUR FACE.
2. THIS HAND IS SIMILAR TO THE HAND ENTITLED "SHUTOUT BID" (NUMBER 15) WHICH APPEARED EARLIER. THIS TIME THE PROBLEM IS PRESENTED FROM THE OTHER DEFENDER'S POINT OF VIEW.
3. NOTE THAT PARTNER COULD AFFORD TO CASH THE ♠A HOLDING A SURE TRUMP TRICK. HE JUST WANTED TO BE SURE THAT YOU DIDN'T LEAD FROM EITHER A DOUBLETON DIAMOND OR J109, HOLDING THE ♠K.

(86) ARE YOU AN EXPERT?

East-West vulnerable
Dealer South

North
♠ K 2
♡ A 10 9 8 2
◊ 10 9 8
♣ 10 9 8

West (you)
♠ J 10 9 3
♡ K 3
◊ Q J 6 5
♣ A Q 7

South	West	North	East
1 ♡	Dbl.	3 ♡	Pass
4 ♡	All Pass		

Opening lead: ♠J

Declarer wins the ♠A, partner playing the ♠8. At trick two declarer leads the ♡Q.

1. Do you cover? Why, or why not?

   You play low and the queen wins, partner following. A second heart is led to the ace, partner discarding the ♣2. The ♠K is cashed, partner playing the ♠4, and the South hand is entered with the ♡J, partner discarding the ♣6.

2. What do you make of the club position?

   Declarer now ruffs a spade in dummy, partner playing the ♠6.

3. What do you make of the spade position?

   The ◊10 is now run to your jack, partner playing the ◊2.

4. What do you play at this point?

ARE YOU AN EXPERT? (Solution)

North
♠ K 2
♡ A 10 9 8 2
◊ 10 9 8
♣ 10 9 8

West
♠ J 10 9 3
♡ K 3
◊ Q J 6 5
♣ A Q 7

East
♠ Q 8 6 4
♡ 4
◊ K 7 2
♣ 6 5 4 3 2

South
♠ A 7 5
♡ Q J 7 6 5
◊ A 4 3
♣ K J

1. Do not cover. What can you promote? Partner is unlikely to have ♡Jx, the only possible reason for covering. Declarer may not even be intending to finesse holding a possible six card suit.
2. Partner's first discard was attitude, his second, present count. By discarding low-high he is showing an *odd* number of worthless clubs. Discarding low-low would show an even number of worthless clubs.
3. Partner must have started with ♠Qxxx.
4. The ◊Q! You have a count and the problem is to avoid leading clubs. If you exit with a low diamond, declarer will win and exit a diamond to your ◊Q. Now you will have to lead clubs. Wonderful. Your unblock allows partner to win the third diamond and his club return through the king defeats the contract one trick.

KEY LESSON POINTERS

1. BEWARE OF COVERING HONORS IN THE TRUMP SUIT UNLESS THERE IS A REASONABLE CHANCE FOR PROMOTION. DECLARER MAY NOT BE INTENDING TO FINESSE.
2. WATCH PARTNER'S DISCARDS LIKE A HAWK. HIS FIRST DISCARD IS USUALLY "ATTITUDE". A SECOND DISCARD IN THE SAME SUIT IS PRESENT COUNT.
3. COUNT EVERY HAND AS IF YOUR LIFE DEPENDED ON IT.

(87) THREE-SUITER?

East-West vulnerable
Dealer South

North
♠ Q 8
♡ J 10 3
♢ A 9 4 3
♣ Q 4 3 2

East (you)
♠ J 7 6 5
♡ A 6 5 4
♢ K 2
♣ 10 7 6

South	West	North	East
1 ♠	Pass	1 NT	Pass
2 ♣	Pass	3 ♣	Pass
3 ♡	Pass	3 ♠	Pass
4 ♠	All Pass		

Opening lead: ♢Q

1. Dummy wins, you play low and declarer plays the ♢10. What is declarer's most likely distribution? Declarer cashes three rounds of spades discarding a club from dummy, while partner discards the ♢5 on the third spade. Declarer continues by playing the ace, king and a club to dummy, partner discarding another diamond on the third club. The ♡J is led from dummy. Your remaining cards are the high trump, the ♢K, and your original heart holding.
2. Which heart do you play? Why?

THREE-SUITER? (Solution)

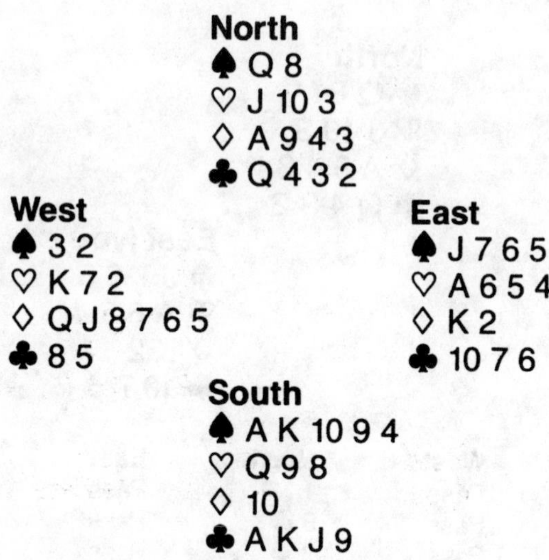

1. 5–3–1–4. With four hearts declarer would have rebid 2♡, not 2♣. There is a slim chance, however, that declarer might have a 6–3–1–3 hand pattern.
2. Declarer has nine tricks outside of hearts and in order to defeat this contract partner must have the ♡K—the ♡Q is not enough. Even so, you must be careful. You must win the first heart play, cash the high spade, and exit a diamond. Declarer will have to ruff with his last trump. When declarer leads a second heart, partner will score his king plus a winning diamond for the setting trick.

   If you duck the heart play and partner wins (either the ♡Q or ♡K), he will exit a diamond which declarer will ruff. Now declarer must come to his tenth trick in hearts because you have no diamond to play upon winning the ♡A.

KEY LESSON POINTERS

1. IF PARTNER NEEDS A PARTICULAR CARD TO DEFEAT THE CONTRACT, ASSUME HE HAS IT.
2. PARTNER'S FIRST DISCARD IN A SUIT IN WHICH HE HAS ORIGINALLY LED AN HONOR IS PRESENT COUNT. IF THE COUNT IS 100% KNOWN, SUIT PREFERENCE TAKES PRECEDENCE (RARE).
3. WHEN PLAYING A FORCING GAME (AS HERE WITH THE DIAMOND SUIT), THE DEFENDER WITH SHORTNESS IN THE DIAMOND SUIT MUST USE HIS ENTRY FIRST.

(88) IT TAKES TWO TO TANGO

North-South vulnerable
Dealer South

North
♠ K J 8
♡ J 7 5 3
◊ A K Q J
♣ K 8

East (you)
♠ 5 2
♡ A Q 4
◊ 7 5 4 3
♣ A J 4 2

South	West	North	East
2 ♠*	Pass	4 ♠	All Pass

*Weak

Opening lead: ♡2

1. Dummy plays low, which heart do you play? Why? What is your plan?
2. You win the ♡Q and return a low heart. Partner wins the ♡K and returns the ♣10. Dummy plays low. Now what is your plan?

IT TAKES TWO TO TANGO (Solution)

North
♠ K J 8
♡ J 7 5 3
◊ A K Q J
♣ K 8

West
♠ 4 3
♡ K 10 2
◊ 10 8 6 2
♣ 10 7 6 5

East
♠ 5 2
♡ A Q 4
◊ 7 5 4 3
♣ A J 4 2

South
♠ A Q 10 9 7 6
♡ 9 8 6
◊ 9
♣ Q 9 3

Clearly your side must try to cash four tricks before declarer draws trumps and enjoys the diamonds.

The problem is that you don't know how many hearts partner has. If he has four, he must hold both the ♡K and the ♣Q to defeat this contract; if he has three, all he needs is the ♡K.

1. To resolve this dilemma it is necessary to play the ♡Q at trick one followed by a low heart. If you play ace and a low heart, partner, holding four hearts, may try to give you a heart ruff. If you play the queen and a low heart, partner will know you have the ♡A and shift to a club.
2. When partner shifts in cash out situations such as this, he will lead low from the queen (or ace) and high from any other holding. Therefore, when partner leads the ♣10 and dummy plays low, rise with the ♣A and hope the ♡A cashes.

KEY LESSON POINTERS

1. DON'T CREATE ANY UNNECESSARY PROBLEMS FOR PARTNER IN CASH OUT SITUATIONS. MAKE YOUR INTENTIONS CRYSTAL CLEAR.
2. WHEN LEADING THROUGH A KING IN A CASH OUT SITUATION, LEAD LOW FROM THE QUEEN OR ACE AND HIGH FROM ANY OTHER HOLDING.
3. ALTHOUGH THE LEAD OF THE LOWEST CARD IN AN UNBID SUIT GENERALLY SHOWS A FOUR CARD SUIT HEADED BY A HIGH HONOR, ALLOWANCES MUST BE MADE FOR A THREE CARD HOLDING.

(89) TOUCHY, TOUCHY

East-West vulnerable
Dealer North

North
♠ K 6
♡ 7 6 5 3
◇ A K 6 2
♣ 10 9 8

East (you)
♠ A J 2
♡ Q 9 8
◇ J 10 9
♣ Q 6 5 4

North	**East**	**South**	**West**
Pass	Pass	1 ◇	Pass
3 ◇	Pass	3 NT	All Pass

Opening lead: ♡2

Your queen goes to declarer's ace. At trick two a low diamond is led to the ace, partner contributing the ◇8, and the ♣10 is passed to partner's king.

1. At trick four partner exits with the ♠10. Declarer plays low from dummy. Which spade do you play? What is your plan?

TOUCHY, TOUCHY (Solution)

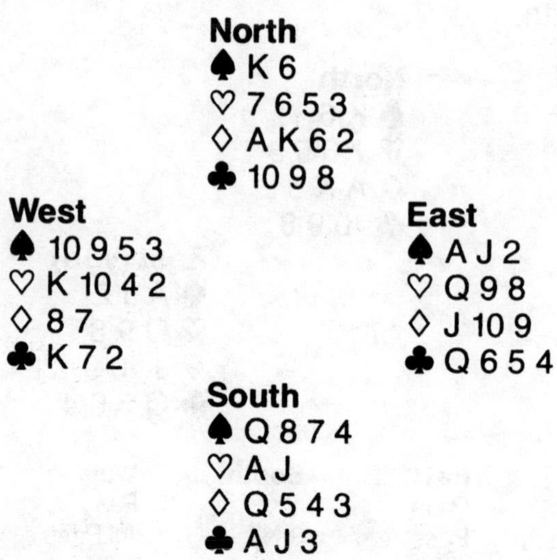

1. Play low. Unless partner's hearts are solid (they can't be; he would have cashed them), the hearts are blocked.

   As long as your main suit is blocked, you must hope that declarer does not have nine tricks after you allow the ♠Q to win. You can survive the play of the ♠J at trick four, but it is not necessary. Showoff.

KEY LESSON POINTERS

1. DON'T PANIC BY MAKING AN UNUSUAL PLAY UNLESS YOU CAN SEE THE SETTING TRICK.
2. WHEN DUMMY HAS FOUR CARDS IN THE SUIT PARTNER HAS LED, AND THIRD HAND HAS A THREE CARD HOLDING WITH GOOD INTERMEDIATE SPOTS, THERE IS SOME CHANCE THAT THE SUIT MAY BE BLOCKED.

(90) NO HELP

East-West vulnerable
Dealer North

North
♠ Q 10 4 2
♡ Q 4
◇ A K 5
♣ K 6 5 3

East (you)
♠ 9
♡ K J 7 6 3
◇ Q 10 9 3
♣ 10 9 7

North	East	South	West
1 ♣	Pass	1 ♠	Pass
2 ♠	Pass	3 ♡	Pass
4 ◇	Pass	6 ♠	All Pass

Opening lead: ♠3

Declarer wins and draws three rounds of trumps as you shed two hearts. Next, declarer plays the ◇AK and ruffs a diamond, finally exiting with the ♡A and ♡10.

1. What is declarer's distribution?
2. What do you return at trick nine? (You are left with a heart, a diamond, and the ♣1097.)

NO HELP (Solution)

	North ♠ Q 10 4 2 ♡ Q 4 ◊ A K 5 ♣ K 6 5 3	
West ♠ 8 5 3 ♡ 9 8 2 ◊ 7 6 4 2 ♣ Q 4 2		East ♠ 9 ♡ K J 7 6 3 ◊ Q 10 9 3 ♣ 10 9 7
	South ♠ A K J 7 6 ♡ A 10 5 ◊ J 8 ♣ A J 8	

1–2. Even without the benefit of any count signals from partner, you know that declarer started with five spades and two diamonds. (He wouldn't be playing the hand like this with four spades.) Declarer remains with either three hearts and three clubs or two hearts and four clubs. At the point you win the ♡K, it really doesn't matter which distribution South had originally. It is perfectly safe to return a heart. Even if you are giving declarer a ruff and sluff, he will still have to deal with the club suit himself.

1–2. If you attack clubs and you find declarer with either AJ8 or AJ8x, you will be giving away a contract that could have been beaten.

If you lead the ♣7, declarer plays the ♣8 intending to finesse the jack later. In this case no finesse will be necessary because the queen will appear. If you attack with the ♣9 or ♣10, declarer can cover and later finesses the ♣8.

KEY LESSON POINTERS

1. DO NOT EXPECT COUNT ON EVERY HAND FROM EVERY PARTNER. LEARN TO MAKE INFERENCES FROM DECLARER'S PLAY. OF COURSE, WHEN DECLARER DOESN'T KNOW WHAT HE IS DOING, THIS CAN LEAD TO SOME HILARIOUS RESULTS.
2. DO NOT AUTOMATICALLY ASSUME THAT A RUFF AND SLUFF IS GOING TO COST A TRICK. IF DECLARER AND DUMMY ARE DIVIDED 4–4 IN THE ALTERNATIVE SUIT, AND THE DEFENDERS' CARDS ARE DIVIDED 3–2, THE RUFF-SLUFF WON'T HURT AND MAY GAIN.

(91) THE WEAK NOTRUMP

East-West vulnerable
Dealer South

North
♠ K Q 4
♡ 10 7 4
♢ Q J 10 7 4
♣ 8 2

East (you)
♠ A 9 8 7
♡ Q 6 5 2
♢ 6 5 3
♣ A 6

South	West	North	East
1 NT*	All Pass		

*12–14

Opening lead: ♣4

You win the ♣A as declarer follows with the ♣5.

1. How many clubs does partner have?
2. What do you return at trick two?

THE WEAK NOTRUMP (Solution)

North
♠ K Q 4
♡ 10 7 4
◇ Q J 10 7 4
♣ 8 2

West
♠ J 5
♡ K J 3
◇ K 8 2
♣ J 10 7 4 3

East
♠ A 9 8 7
♡ Q 6 5 2
◇ 6 5 3
♣ A 6

South
♠ 10 6 3 2
♡ A 9 8
◇ A 9
♣ K Q 9 5

1. Four or five depending upon who has the ♣3.
2. The ♠7. Although there are a number of attractive possibilities, most important is to try to kill the entry to dummy's diamonds in case partner has a diamond honor or declarer has ◇AK blank.

   In order for this play to succeed, you must find your partner with the ♠J and any three diamonds. This appears better than returning partner's suit knowing declarer has at least four clubs. If you can get rid of one of those spade honors, dummy's diamonds may well be worthless. In fact, your return holds declarer to six tricks even if he guesses NOT to play the ♠10 at trick two.

KEY LESSON POINTERS

1. WHEN TRYING TO COUNT THE NUMBER OF CARDS PARTNER HAS IN THE SUIT HE HAS LED, LOOK BENEATH THE CARD THAT WAS LED. IF YOU CAN SEE ALL OF THE LOWER SPOTS YOU KNOW YOUR PARTNER STARTED WITH A FOUR CARD SUIT. IF ONE LOWER SPOT IS MISSING PARTNER MAY HAVE STARTED WITH A FIVE CARD SUIT—OR DECLARER MAY ACTUALLY BE WITHHOLDING THE LOWER SPOT TO TRY TO CONFUSE A GREAT PLAYER LIKE YOU.
2. WHEN DUMMY HAS AN ESTABLISHABLE SUIT, TRY TO REMOVE THE OUTSIDE ENTRY BEFORE THE SUIT CAN BE SET UP.

(92) CUE BID RAISE

East-West vulnerable
Dealer East

North
♠ Q 6 5 3
♡ J 10 7 6 4
◇ K 4
♣ Q 9

East (you)
♠ 7 5 2
♡ A K 8
◇ A 7 3 2
♣ 10 5 3

East	**South**	**West**	**North**
Pass	1 ◇	1 ♠	Dbl.*
2 ◇**	3 ♣	Pass	3 ◇
All Pass			

*Negative
**Strong spade raise

Opening lead: ♠K

You play low and declarer follows with the ♠8. Partner shifts to the ♡5 which you win with the ♡K, declarer playing the ♡Q.

1. What do you play to trick three? Why?
   You cash the ♡A, partner follows with the ♡3 and declarer the ♡9.
2. What do you play to trick four?

CUE BID RAISE (Solution)

North
♠ Q 6 5 3
♡ J 10 7 6 4
◊ K 4
♣ Q 9

West
♠ A K J 10 9
♡ 5 3 2
◊ 9 6
♣ J 4 2

East
♠ 7 5 2
♡ A K 8
◊ A 7 3 2
♣ 10 5 3

South
♠ 8
♡ Q 9
◊ Q J 10 8 5
♣ A K 8 7 6

1. The second heart must cash. With four hearts partner would normally lead low. Besides, declarer is unlikely to hold two major suit singletons.
2. A spade. Partner may or may not be able to ruff the heart, but the spade return insures a set. If declarer ruffs he will be down to four trumps. When you get in with the ace of trump you will play another spade. Declarer will have to ruff again and your long trump becomes the setting trick.

KEY LESSON POINTERS

1. WHEN LEADING THE TOP OF THREE SMALL, PLAY THE MIDDLE CARD NEXT. PLAYING THE LOWEST SHOWS A DOUBLETON OR, IN CERTAIN CASES, FOUR CARDS.
2. WHEN HOLDING FOUR TRUMPS LOOK AROUND FOR A WAY TO SHORTEN DECLARER'S TRUMP HOLDING AND, PERHAPS, ESTABLISH A LONG TRUMP FOR YOURSELF.
3. IF IN THE SUIT YOU ARE FORCING DECLARER TO RUFF (IN THIS CASE SPADES), DECLARER HAS A DELAYED WINNER (THE QUEEN), IT MAY BE NECESSARY TO CASH YOUR SIDE SUIT WINNERS FIRST. IF YOU PLAY A SPADE BEFORE CASHING THE SECOND HEART, DECLARER WILL DISCARD A HEART AND BE ABLE TO AVOID TWO FORCES.

(93) DIRECTIONAL ASKING BID

Neither side vulnerable
Dealer North

North
♠ J 10 6
♡ A K J 5 3
♢ A Q 8 4
♣ 2

East (you)
♠ Q 8 4 3
♡ Q 10 9 7
♢ 9 6
♣ 9 5 4

North	**East**	**South**	**West**
1 ♡	Pass	2 ♣	Pass
2 ♢	Pass	3 ♣*	Pass
3 ♠**	Pass	3 NT	All Pass

*Invitational
**Asking for a spade stopper

Opening lead: ♠2

1. Dummy plays the ♠10. Which spade do you play? Why?

DIRECTIONAL ASKING BID (Solution)

North
♠ J 10 6
♡ A K J 5 3
◇ A Q 8 4
♣ 2

West
♠ K 9 7 2
♡ 8 6
◇ K 10 5 2
♣ A 10 3

East
♠ Q 8 4 3
♡ Q 10 9 7
◇ 9 6
♣ 9 5 4

South
♠ A 5
♡ 4 2
◇ J 7 3
♣ K Q J 8 7 6

1. The ♠Q. Under normal circumstances you should simply signal with the ♠8. If declarer has ♠Kx you save a trick by NOT playing the ♠Q. However, there are other considerations, namely removing declarer's entry prematurely before the club suit can be established.

   You must assume that partner has at least one club stopper. How will declarer get back to his hand to use his clubs? Certainly not in hearts. If partner has the ◇K, there is no way back other than in spades.

   Even though you may be sacrificing a spade trick (if partner has the ♠A), your greater concern is with killing the club suit.

KEY LESSON POINTERS

1. WHEN THIRD HAND HAS THE QUEEN AND DUMMY J10x, IT IS NOT ALWAYS CLEAR WHICH CARD TO PLAY WHEN PARTNER LEADS LOW VS. NOTRUMP. IF:
   (a) DECLARER HAS Kx IT IS RIGHT TO SIGNAL.
   (b) IF PARTNER HAS BOTH THE ACE AND KING IT IS NOT ONLY RIGHT TO PLAY THE QUEEN, IT IS HEALTHIER.
   (c) IF IT IS NECESSARY TO REMOVE A DECLARER HAND ENTRY, THE QUEEN MUST BE PLAYED.
   (d) IF IT IS IMPORTANT TO KILL A LATER DUMMY ENTRY, A SIGNAL SHOULD BE GIVEN.
   (e) IT IS USUALLY RIGHT NOT TO PLAY THE QUEEN. HELP!

(94) WEAK PARTNER

Neither side vulnerable
Dealer South

North
♠ 7 5 4
♡ K 8 7
♢ Q J 10 3
♣ A K 7

East (you)
♠ A 8 6
♡ 4 3 2
♢ K 6 5
♣ Q 5 4 2

South	West	North	East
1 ♡	Pass	2 ♢	Pass
2 ♡	Pass	4 ♡	All Pass

Opening lead: ♠J (Denies a higher honor)

1. Which card to you play at trick one? Why?
2. You win the ♠A, declarer playing the ♠2. What do you return at trick two?

   You return the ♣2. Declarer plays the ♣9, partner the ♣J and dummy wins. Declarer plays the ♡AQ, partner following, and leads the ♢4. Partner plays the ♢9, and you capture dummy's 10.
3. What do you return?

WEAK PARTNER (Solution)

	North	
	♠ 7 5 4 ♡ K 8 7 ♢ Q J 10 3 ♣ A K 7	
West ♠ J 10 9 3 ♡ 6 5 ♢ A 9 8 7 ♣ J 8 6		**East** ♠ A 8 6 ♡ 4 3 2 ♢ K 6 5 ♣ Q 5 4 2
	South ♠ K Q 2 ♡ A Q J 10 9 ♢ 4 2 ♣ 10 9 3	

1. The ♠A. Declarer is known to hold the ♠KQ and your plan should be to try to establish a club winner before declarer sets up the diamonds. You know that declarer is looking at a likely nine tricks: five hearts, two spades and two clubs.
2. A low club.
3. Another low club. Declarer is known to have the ♣10, but you have no alternative. If you lead a second low club declarer may misguess and play low. Partner's ♣8 will then drive out dummy's remaining high honor and your queen will be established as the setting trick.

   Your partner, of course, has made a horrendous play by not winning the first diamond and leading a club in which case declarer would have no chance. Time to think about a new partner—this one is too busy giving lovely count signals rather than playing bridge.

KEY LESSON POINTERS

1. IF YOU CAN SEE THAT THE SETTING TRICK MUST COME FROM A PARTICULAR SUIT, AND THERE IS A TIME ELEMENT INVOLVED, ATTACK THAT SUIT AT ONCE.
2. ON THIS HAND, THE LEAD OF THE JACK DENYING A HIGHER HONOR IS HELPFUL TO THE DEFENSE.
3. SOME PARTNERS ARE SO BUSY SIGNALLING COUNT, THAT THEY FORGET TO PLAY BRIDGE. (WEST'S PLAY OF THE ♢9 INSTEAD OF THE ♢A).

(95) CAREFUL CARDING

North-South vulnerable
Dealer South

North
♠ K Q 10
♡ A 4 3 2
◇ K Q
♣ J 8 5 3

West (you)
♠ 7 4 3
♡ 9 6
◇ J 10 8 7 6
♣ 10 9 7

South	West	North	East
1 NT	Pass	2 ♣	Pass
2 ♡*	Pass	4 ◇**	Pass
6 ♡	All Pass		

*Does not deny four spades
**Balanced slam try in hearts

Opening lead: ◇J

Partner plays the ◇5 and declarer wins with the ◇A. At trick two the ♡Q loses to partner's K. Partner returns the ◇2.

1. If you want to show your partner an original holding of five diamonds (you seldom give honest count against slams), which diamond would you play?
2. Declarer draws two more rounds of trumps ending in dummy, partner following. What do you discard on the third round of trumps?
3. What are declarer's two most likely distributions?
4. Declarer leads a low club from dummy, partner plays the ♣2 and declarer the ♣Q. Which club do you play? Why?

CAREFUL CARDING (Solution)

North
♠ K Q 10
♡ A 4 3 2
◊ K Q
♣ J 8 5 3

West
♠ 7 4 3
♡ 9 6
◊ J 10 8 7 6
♣ 10 9 7

East
♠ J 9 8 2
♡ K 8 5
◊ 9 5 4 2
♣ K 2

South
♠ A 6 5
♡ Q J 10 7
◊ A 3
♣ A Q 6 4

1. The ◊8. To give count in a long suit after having led an honor, play high the second time to show an original holding of five cards and low to show an original holding of four or six cards.
2. A diamond. In general, it pays to discard from nonimportant length to avoid showing out in a side suit later in the play, thus making you a lifelong friend of the declarer.
3. Either 4–4–2–3 or 3–4–2–4.
4. The ♣9 or the ♣10. If declarer has four spades and three clubs the hand is unmakeable whenever partner has the ♣K. However, if declarer has four clubs and partner ♣Kx, you must play the ♣9 or ♣10 to give declarer an option in the play. If declarer thinks you started with ♣109 doubleton, he will enter dummy and lead the ♣J, just what you want him to do. Partner will, perforce, cover and you will have the setting trick in clubs. If you play the ♣7 under the ♣Q, declarer has no choice but to bang down the ♣A.

KEY LESSON POINTERS

1. BE PRUDENT ABOUT GIVING PARTNER COUNT VS. A SLAM. HOWEVER, IF ONE PLAYER IS GOING TO TELL THE TRUTH, IT SHOULD BE THE WEAKER HAND.
2. IN GENERAL, DISCARD FROM LENGTH RATHER THAN SHORTNESS. DISCARDING FROM SHORTNESS GIVES THE DECLARER TOO MUCH INFORMATION WHEN YOU SHOW OUT OF A SUIT. PARTNER'S HONOR HOLDING IS NOW EXPOSED IN THE SUIT.
3. TRY TO GIVE DECLARER A LOSING OPTION IN THE PLAY WHEN HIS NORMAL PLAY WILL SUCCEED. AN EXAMPLE IS PLAYING THE ♣9 OR ♣10 FROM 109x.

(96) POURING IT ON

Neither side vulnerable
Dealer North

North
♠ A 3 2
♡ K Q 3
◊ 5 4
♣ Q J 10 8 4

West (you)
♠ J 9 8 4
♡ J 10 8 7
◊ 9 3
♣ A 7 2

North	East	South	West
1 ♣	1 ◊	2 NT*	Pass
3 NT	All Pass		

*13 – 15 – does not deny a four card major.

Opening lead: ◊9

Partner plays the ◊10 and declarer the ◊J. At trick two declarer leads a low club. It's your turn.

1. Should you be spectacular and play the ace, or should you play low?
2. Assume you play the ♣A, what do you play at trick three?

POURING IT ON (Solution)

	North	
	♠ A 3 2 ♡ K Q 3 ♢ 5 4 ♣ Q J 10 8 4	
West ♠ J 9 8 4 ♡ J 10 8 7 ♢ 9 3 ♣ A 7 2		**East** ♠ Q 10 5 ♡ 6 5 ♢ A 10 8 7 6 2 ♣ K 3
	South ♠ K 7 6 ♡ A 9 4 2 ♢ K Q J ♣ 9 6 5	

1. You should play the ♣A, and it is *not* a spectacular play. Your partner has signalled you at trick one that he likes diamonds. It is important that the hand shorter in the suit being established—diamonds—wins the early lead. In that way the hand with the longer diamonds can retain an entry to run the suit after it has been established.
2. Your other diamond—but only if you wish to continue playing with this particular partner. If you can't stand him, shift to a major.

KEY LESSON POINTERS

1. THIRD HAND FREQUENTLY MUST MAINTAIN COMMUNICATIONS WITH PARTNER'S HAND BY MAKING AN EARLY DUCKING PLAY IN HIS LONG SUIT.
2. IT IS A PRINCIPLE OF NOTRUMP DEFENSE THAT THE PLAYER WITH THE SHORTER HOLDING IN THE SUIT THE DEFENDERS ARE TRYING TO SET UP USE HIS OUTSIDE ENTRY FIRST.
3. WHEN NOT SURE ABOUT THE POINT COUNT OR DISTRIBUTION OF A PARTICULAR BID, INQUIRE BEFORE YOU LEAD. FOR EXAMPLE, SOME PLAY THAT A 2NT JUMP RESPONSE IN COMPETITION IS NOT FORCING. OTHERS PLAY THAT IT DENIES A FOUR CARD MAJOR. YOU ARE ENTITLED TO THIS INFORMATION.

(97) 8 FOR STARTERS

Neither side vulnerable
Dealer North

North
♠ A
♡ 9 2
◇ A K Q J 9 8
♣ A 10 7 3

East (you)
♠ Q 10 8
♡ A K 7 6 3
◇ 10 7 3
♣ K 5

North	East	South	West
1 ◇	1 ♡	1 ♠*	Pass
3 ♣	Pass	3 NT	All Pass

*Guarantees at least five spades

Opening lead: ♡10

1. Dummy plays low, which heart do you play?
   You win the ♡K. You are not about to give them their ninth trick at trick one, are you? Please God.
2. What do you play at trick two? Why?
   You cash the ♡A and partner discards the ♠2.
3. What is declarer's distribution?
4. What do you play to trick three?

8 FOR STARTERS (Solution)

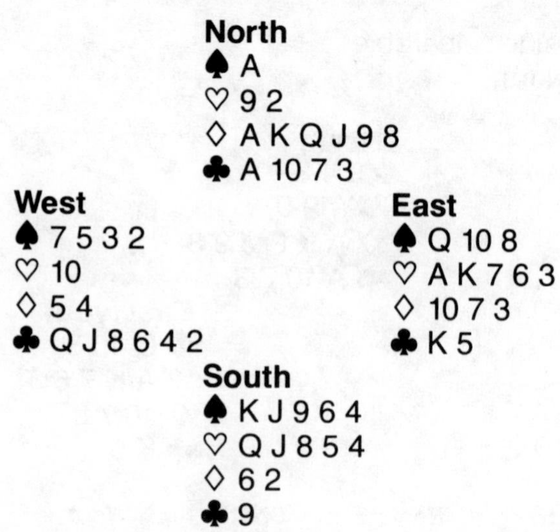

1–2. It can't hurt to cash the ♡A, and if partner discards, you might get some helpful information.

3. Declarer is known to have at least 10 major suit cards but you can't be sure about his minor suit distribution, although he is unlikely to be void in clubs (he probably would bid 3◊ over 3♣ with 5–5–3–0 distribution).

4. Inasmuch as declarer has the ♠K (judging from partner's discard), partner needs both the ♣QJ to defeat this contract. Even so, you must shift to the ♣K right now or else you won't be able to untangle yourself from the four card end position that will develop.

   Notice that if you play the ♣K declarer is helpless. If he ducks, you continue the suit. Later partner must make two more club tricks. If dummy wins the ♣A, partner makes the last three club tricks.

   This is what will happen if you exit passively: Declarer will run off all of his winners reducing to four clubs in the dummy. You will remain with ♣Kx and two major suit losers and partner with four clubs. Declarer will lead a low club from dummy. If you rise and return a club, declarer will duck endplaying your partner. If you duck the club, partner will win and exit a club which declarer will duck to your king. You will now have to concede the last two tricks to declarer's major suit winners.

KEY LESSON POINTERS

1. REALIZING THAT DECLARER MAY HAVE INSOLUBLE ENTRY PROBLEMS IS THE MARK OF A STRONG DEFENDER.
2. WHEN IT SEEMS APPARENT THAT THE DUMMY CAN BE LOCKED IN, TRY TO REMOVE ALL OF THE SAFE EXIT CARDS FROM DUMMY EARLY. FOR EXAMPLE, CASHING THE SECOND HEART REMOVES DUMMY'S SAFEST EXIT.

(98) ALPHONSE AND GASTON

North-South vulnerable
Dealer South

North
♠ 9 4 3
♡ A 10 9
◊ Q 10 7 6
♣ Q 10 9

West (you)
♠ Q 8 2
♡ 5 4 3 2
◊ A 8 2
♣ 6 5 3

South	West	North	East
1 NT	Pass	2 NT	Pass
3 NT	All Pass		

Opening lead: ♠2

Partner wins the ♠K and continues with the ♠A, declarer following with the ♠6 and the ♠J.

1. Which spade do you play under the ace? Why?

ALPHONSE AND GASTON (Solution)

North
♠ 9 4 3
♡ A 10 9
♢ Q 10 7 6
♣ Q 10 9

West
♠ Q 8 2
♡ 5 4 3 2
♢ A 8 2
♣ 6 5 3

East
♠ A K 7
♡ 8 7 6
♢ K 4 3
♣ 8 7 4 2

South
♠ J 10 6 5
♡ K Q J
♢ J 9 5
♣ A K J

1. Do not unblock! Play the ♠8. If partner wanted you to unblock he would have played his spade honors in reverse order— first the ace and then the king.

KEY LESSON POINTERS

1. PLAYING HONORS OUT OF ORDER ON DEFENSE (HIGHER-LOWER) SHOWS A DOUBLETON AT SUIT CONTRACTS, BUT ASKS FOR AN UNBLOCK AT NOTRUMP.

North
♠ A 9 3

West
♠ J 8 7 6 4

East
♠ K Q

South
♠ 10 5 2

VS. SUIT WEST LEADS THE ♠6. ASSUMING DUMMY PLAYS LOW, EAST WINS WITH THE ♠K AND RETURNS THE ♠Q TO SHOW A DOUBLETON. EVEN IF DUMMY PLAYS THE ACE ORIGINALLY, EAST SHOULD PLAY THE KING.

North
♠ J 10

West
♠ 9 8 2

East
♠ K Q 7 6 3

South
♠ A 5 4

VS. NOTRUMP WEST LEADS THE ♠9. EAST, WITHOUT AN OUTSIDE ENTRY, COVERS WITH THE KING. ASSUMING THIS HOLDS, EAST CONTINUES WITH THE ♠Q ASKING FOR AN UNBLOCK. IF EAST PLAYS THE QUEEN AND THEN THE KING, (NORMAL ORDER) WEST SHOULD NOT UNBLOCK.

(99) GIVING THEM A SECOND CHANCE

Neither side vulnerable
Dealer South

North
♠ 5 3
♡ 6
◊ K 9 8 7 6 4 2
♣ J 5 4

West (you)
♠ Q 10 7 6
♡ 10 4
◊ Q 10 3
♣ A 7 6 2

South	West	North	East
1 ♡	Pass	Pass	2 ♣
4 ♡	All Pass		

Opening lead: ♣A

Partner plays the ♣9 and declarer the ♣10.

1. What do you play next?

GIVING THEM A SECOND CHANCE (Solution)

North
♠ 5 3
♡ 6
♢ K 9 8 7 6 4 2
♣ J 5 4

West
♠ Q 10 7 6
♡ 10 4
♢ Q 10 3
♣ A 7 6 2

East
♠ 9 8 2
♡ A J 5
♢ J 5
♣ K Q 9 8 3

South
♠ A K J 4
♡ K Q 9 8 7 3 2
♢ A
♣ 10

1. The ♡10. Partner has signalled you encouragement in clubs, but he doesn't know you have four clubs.

   From your point of view declarer cannot use the diamond suit, but there is a chance that he may be able to ruff a spade in dummy if he has the ♠AK.

   Returning a low trump chews up one of your natural trump tricks, but does defeat the hand one trick. You will still get two more spades and one heart. However, the proper return of the ♡10 will defeat the contract two tricks as you will wind up taking two tricks in each major along with the ♣A. If you fail to play a heart at trick two, declarer makes the hand by cashing the ♢A, ruffing a spade, and discarding a spade on the ♢K. Now only two more trump tricks must be lost.

KEY LESSON POINTERS

1. WHEN DUMMY HAS A WORTHLESS LONG SUIT BUT A POSSIBLE RUFFING VALUE IT IS USUALLY RIGHT TO PLAY A TRUMP.
2. HOLDING 10x OR Jx AND LEADING INTO A STRONG TRUMP HOLDING WITH AN ENTRYLESS DUMMY, IT IS BETTER TO LEAD THE HONOR IN CASE PARTNER HAS ONE OR TWO HONORS IN THE SUIT.
3. PARTNER'S TRICK ONE ATTITUDE SIGNAL IS NOT INVIOLABLE. WHEN YOU KNOW SOMETHING HE CAN'T KNOW, YOU ARE ALLOWED TO TAKE CHARGE.

(100) ENDING ON A SWEET NOTE

East-West vulnerable
Dealer South

North
♠ J 5
♡ 10 9 3 2
◊ J 7 3
♣ Q J 10 9

West (you)
♠ A K Q 8 3
♡ J 7 4
◊ 6 2
♣ K 7 4

South	West	North	East
2 NT*	**Pass**	**3 ♣**	Pass
3 ♡	Pass	4 ♡	All Pass

*20 – 21

Opening lead: ♠Q

Partner plays the ♠2, count, declarer plays the ♠4.

1. What is your game plan, and what do you continue at trick two?

   You continue with the ♠A and ♠K, declarer ruffing in dummy, partner and declarer following. The ♣Q is led from dummy, partner plays the ♣2, declarer the ♣5.

2. What is declarer's distribution?
3. Do you win this trick? If so, what do you return? If not, why not?

ENDING ON A SWEET NOTE (Solution)

North
♠ J 5
♡ 10 9 3 2
◇ J 7 3
♣ Q J 10 9

West
♠ A K Q 8 3
♡ J 7 4
◇ 6 2
♣ K 7 4

East
♠ 9 6 2
♡ 8 5
◇ Q 10 9 5 4
♣ 8 6 2

South
♠ 10 7 4
♡ A K Q 6
◇ A K 8
♣ A 5 3

1. Your plan should be to kill dummy's club suit by forcing declarer to use dummy's lone entry prematurely (the fourth trump), before the clubs can be established.
2. 3–4–3–3. Partner has given you count in both black suits, and unless declarer has a five card heart suit his distribution is a read-out.
3. You should duck the trick. You know from partner's count signal that declarer has ♣Axx. If you win the trick declarer will be able to use one of dummy's clubs to discard a losing diamond. If you duck the trick, declarer will have to lose a club as well as a diamond trick.

KEY LESSON POINTERS

1. FORCING THE DUMMY TO RUFF EARLY IS ONE WAY OF KILLING DUMMY'S LENGTH IN WHICH EITHER YOU OR PARTNER HAS A STOPPER.
2. HOLDING Kxx WITH THE QJ10x TO YOUR LEFT, IT IS OFTEN RIGHT TO DUCK THE QUEEN WHEN PARTNER SHOWS YOU THREE CARDS IN THE SUIT. IF DECLARER REPEATS THE FINESSE YOU WIN AND THE SUIT IS BLOCKED. IF DECLARER PLAYS ACE AND ANOTHER, HE MAY NOT BE ABLE TO GET TO DUMMY'S ESTABLISHED THIRTEENER. IF YOU TAKE THE FIRST TRICK, DECLARER GETS THREE EASY TRICKS IN THE SUIT.

APPENDIX (Themes)

1. Reading the Lead — Trump Echo
2. Killing an Entry — Helping Partner to Avoid an Error
3. Preventing a Hold-Up Play by Declarer
4. Card Combinations
5. Making the Killing Shift
6. Reading Partner's Attitude Signals
7. Applying the Rule of 11-Counting Tricks — Leading an Unsuppported Honor
8. Forcing Declarer to Ruff While Allowing Partner to Discard a Loser.
9. Giving a Ruff and Sluff for Trump Promotion
10. Counting Declarer's Distribution
11. Inferring Declarer's Distribution
12. Reading an Unblock
13. Card Combinations — Exiting Safely
14. Avoiding an Endplay
15. Giving Yourself Two Chances
16. Killing Dummy's Length
17. Going for a Ruff
18. Counting Declarer's Tricks — Reading an Unusual Honor Play
19. Counting Declarer's Distribution — Going for a Ruff
20. Simplifying the Defense
21. Card Combinations — Reading the Lead — Negative Discarding
22. Overtaking Partner's Lead to Make the Killing Shift
23. Killing Dummy's Long Suit While Retaining Control — Counting Tricks
24. Unblocking
25. Deception
26. Reading the Distribution — Giving Partner a Ruff
27. Playing the Forcing Game
28. Getting a Ruff
29. Killing an Entry
30. Trump Promotion — The Uppercut — Card Combinations
31. Giving Partner a Ruff While Retaining Control of the Suit
32. Second Hand High — Counting Tricks
33. Getting Partner Off an Endplay
34. Getting a Ruff by Leading a Trump
35. Playing the Odds
36. Killing Dummy's Entry to a Long Suit

37. Counting Tricks — Card Combinations
38. Honor Signalling
39. Recognizing a Suit Preference Signal — Cashing Out
40. Taking Charge of the Defense
41. Card Combinations
42. Counting Tricks — Unblocking for Partner — Card Combinations
43. Killing a Dummy Entry
44. Getting Partner off an Endplay
45. Counting Declarer's Points — Placing the Missing Honors
46. Blocking a Long Suit by Leading a High Honor from Honor Third
47. Ruffing Partner's Trick — Card Combinations — Leading an Unsupported Honor
48. Trump Promotion — Refusing an Overruff
49. Killing a Dummy Entry — Counting Tricks
50. Third Hand PLay — False Attitude Signal at Trick One
51. Giving Partner a Ruff
52. Card Combinations
53. Playing Honors Out of Order — Counting Tricks
54. Inferences — Card Combinations
55. Hold-Up in the Trump Suit
56. Preventing Declarer from Leading from Dummy to Take a Winning Finesse — Placing the Cards
57. Trump Management with Axx
58. Playing For the Sure Set
59. Second Hand High — Giving the Declarer a Losing Option
60. Trump Management — Entry Considerations
61. Giving Partner a Ruff While Retaining Control of the Suit
62. Getting a Ruff — Ducking Play in the Trump Suit
63. Avoiding a Trump Coup — Removing a Dummy Entry Prematurely
64. Second Hand Play — Avoiding a Throw-In
65. Giving Yourself Two Chances
66. Overtaking Partner's Trick — Card Combinations
67. Getting a Ruff by Giving a Ruff and Sluff
68. Unblocking to Avoid an Endplay
69. Killing Dummy's Long Suit — Counting Tricks
70. Taking the Sure Set
71. Reading a Suit Preference Signal
72. Reading an Unblock from Partner

MELVIN POWERS SELF-IMPROVEMENT LIBRARY

ASTROLOGY

____ ASTROLOGY: HOW TO CHART YOUR HOROSCOPE *Max Heindel* 5.00
____ ASTROLOGY AND SEXUAL ANALYSIS *Morris C. Goodman* 5.00
____ ASTROLOGY MADE EASY *Astarte* 3.00
____ ASTROLOGY MADE PRACTICAL *Alexandra Kayhle* 3.00
____ ASTROLOGY, ROMANCE, YOU AND THE STARS *Anthony Norvell* 5.00
____ MY WORLD OF ASTROLOGY *Sydney Omarr* 7.00
____ THOUGHT DIAL *Sydney Omarr* 4.00
____ WHAT THE STARS REVEAL ABOUT THE MEN IN YOUR LIFE *Thelma White* 3.00

BRIDGE

____ BRIDGE BIDDING MADE EASY *Edwin B. Kantar* 10.00
____ BRIDGE CONVENTIONS *Edwin B. Kantar* 7.00
____ BRIDGE HUMOR *Edwin B. Kantar* 5.00
____ COMPETITIVE BIDDING IN MODERN BRIDGE *Edgar Kaplan* 7.00
____ DEFENSIVE BRIDGE PLAY COMPLETE *Edwin B. Kantar* 15.00
____ GAMESMAN BRIDGE—Play Better with Kantar *Edwin B. Kantar* 5.00
____ HOW TO IMPROVE YOUR BRIDGE *Alfred Sheinwold* 5.00
____ IMPROVING YOUR BIDDING SKILLS *Edwin B. Kantar* 4.00
____ INTRODUCTION TO DECLARER'S PLAY *Edwin B. Kantar* 5.00
____ INTRODUCTION TO DEFENDER'S PLAY *Edwin B. Kantar* 3.00
____ KANTAR FOR THE DEFENSE *Edwin B. Kantar* 7.00
____ KANTAR FOR THE DEFENSE VOLUME 2 *Edwin B. Kantar* 7.00
____ SHORT CUT TO WINNING BRIDGE *Alfred Sheinwold* 3.00
____ TEST YOUR BRIDGE PLAY *Edwin B. Kantar* 5.00
____ VOLUME 2—TEST YOUR BRIDGE PLAY *Edwin B. Kantar* 5.00
____ WINNING DECLARER PLAY *Dorothy Hayden Truscott* 5.00

BUSINESS, STUDY & REFERENCE

____ CONVERSATION MADE EASY *Elliot Russell* 4.00
____ EXAM SECRET *Dennis B. Jackson* 3.00
____ FIX-IT BOOK *Arthur Symons* 2.00
____ HOW TO DEVELOP A BETTER SPEAKING VOICE *M. Hellier* 4.00
____ HOW TO SELF-PUBLISH YOUR BOOK & MAKE IT A BEST SELLER *Melvin Powers* 10.00
____ INCREASE YOUR LEARNING POWER *Geoffrey A. Dudley* 3.00
____ PRACTICAL GUIDE TO BETTER CONCENTRATION *Melvin Powers* 3.00
____ PRACTICAL GUIDE TO PUBLIC SPEAKING *Maurice Forley* 5.00
____ 7 DAYS TO FASTER READING *William S. Schaill* 5.00
____ SONGWRITERS' RHYMING DICTIONARY *Jane Shaw Whitfield* 7.00
____ SPELLING MADE EASY *Lester D. Basch & Dr. Milton Finkelstein* 3.00
____ STUDENT'S GUIDE TO BETTER GRADES *J. A. Rickard* 3.00
____ TEST YOURSELF—Find Your Hidden Talent *Jack Shafer* 3.00
____ YOUR WILL & WHAT TO DO ABOUT IT *Attorney Samuel G. Kling* 5.00

CALLIGRAPHY

____ ADVANCED CALLIGRAPHY *Katherine Jeffares* 7.00
____ CALLIGRAPHER'S REFERENCE BOOK *Anne Leptich & Jacque Evans* 7.00
____ CALLIGRAPHY—The Art of Beautiful Writing *Katherine Jeffares* 7.00
____ CALLIGRAPHY FOR FUN & PROFIT *Anne Leptich & Jacque Evans* 7.00
____ CALLIGRAPHY MADE EASY *Tina Serafini* 7.00

CHESS & CHECKERS

____ BEGINNER'S GUIDE TO WINNING CHESS *Fred Reinfeld* 5.00
____ CHESS IN TEN EASY LESSONS *Larry Evans* 5.00
____ CHESS MADE EASY *Milton L. Hanauer* 3.00
____ CHESS PROBLEMS FOR BEGINNERS *edited by Fred Reinfeld* 2.00
____ CHESS SECRETS REVEALED *Fred Reinfeld* 2.00
____ CHESS TACTICS FOR BEGINNERS *edited by Fred Reinfeld* 5.00
____ CHESS THEORY & PRACTICE *Morry & Mitchell* 2.00
____ HOW TO WIN AT CHECKERS *Fred Reinfeld* 3.00
____ 1001 BRILLIANT WAYS TO CHECKMATE *Fred Reinfeld* 5.00
____ 1001 WINNING CHESS SACRIFICES & COMBINATIONS *Fred Reinfeld* 5.00
____ SOVIET CHESS *Edited by R. G. Wade* 3.00

COOKERY & HERBS

____	CULPEPER'S HERBAL REMEDIES *Dr. Nicholas Culpeper*	3.00
____	FAST GOURMET COOKBOOK *Poppy Cannon*	2.50
____	GINSENG The Myth & The Truth *Joseph P. Hou*	3.00
____	HEALING POWER OF HERBS *May Bethel*	4.00
____	HEALING POWER OF NATURAL FOODS *May Bethel*	5.00
____	HERB HANDBOOK *Dawn MacLeod*	3.00
____	HERBS FOR HEALTH—How to Grow & Use Them *Louise Evans Doole*	4.00
____	HOME GARDEN COOKBOOK—Delicious Natural Food Recipes *Ken Kraft*	3.00
____	MEDICAL HERBALIST *edited by Dr. J. R. Yemm*	3.00
____	VEGETABLE GARDENING FOR BEGINNERS *Hugh Wiberg*	2.00
____	VEGETABLES FOR TODAY'S GARDENS *R. Milton Carleton*	2.00
____	VEGETARIAN COOKERY *Janet Walker*	4.00
____	VEGETARIAN COOKING MADE EASY & DELECTABLE *Veronica Vezza*	3.00
____	VEGETARIAN DELIGHTS—A Happy Cookbook for Health *K. R. Mehta*	2.00
____	VEGETARIAN GOURMET COOKBOOK *Joyce McKinnel*	3.00

GAMBLING & POKER

____	ADVANCED POKER STRATEGY & WINNING PLAY *A. D. Livingston*	5.00
____	HOW TO WIN AT DICE GAMES *Skip Frey*	3.00
____	HOW TO WIN AT POKER *Terence Reese & Anthony T. Watkins*	5.00
____	WINNING AT CRAPS *Dr. Lloyd T. Commins*	4.00
____	WINNING AT GIN *Chester Wander & Cy Rice*	3.00
____	WINNING AT POKER—An Expert's Guide *John Archer*	5.00
____	WINNING AT 21—An Expert's Guide *John Archer*	5.00
____	WINNING POKER SYSTEMS *Norman Zadeh*	3.00

HEALTH

____	BEE POLLEN *Lynda Lyngheim & Jack Scagnetti*	3.00
____	DR. LINDNER'S SPECIAL WEIGHT CONTROL METHOD *P. G. Lindner, M.D.*	2.00
____	HELP YOURSELF TO BETTER SIGHT *Margaret Darst Corbett*	3.00
____	HOW TO IMPROVE YOUR VISION *Dr. Robert A. Kraskin*	3.00
____	HOW YOU CAN STOP SMOKING PERMANENTLY *Ernest Caldwell*	3.00
____	MIND OVER PLATTER *Peter G. Lindner, M.D.*	3.00
____	NATURE'S WAY TO NUTRITION & VIBRANT HEALTH *Robert J. Scrutton*	3.00
____	NEW CARBOHYDRATE DIET COUNTER *Patti Lopez-Pereira*	2.00
____	QUICK & EASY EXERCISES FOR FACIAL BEAUTY *Judy Smith-deal*	2.00
____	QUICK & EASY EXERCISES FOR FIGURE BEAUTY *Judy Smith-deal*	2.00
____	REFLEXOLOGY *Dr. Maybelle Segal*	4.00
____	REFLEXOLOGY FOR GOOD HEALTH *Anna Kaye & Don C. Matchan*	5.00
____	30 DAYS TO BEAUTIFUL LEGS *Dr. Marc Selner*	3.00
____	YOU CAN LEARN TO RELAX *Dr. Samuel Gutwirth*	3.00
____	YOUR ALLERGY—What To Do About It *Allan Knight, M.D.*	3.00

HOBBIES

____	BEACHCOMBING FOR BEGINNERS *Norman Hickin*	2.00
____	BLACKSTONE'S MODERN CARD TRICKS *Harry Blackstone*	3.00
____	BLACKSTONE'S SECRETS OF MAGIC *Harry Blackstone*	3.00
____	COIN COLLECTING FOR BEGINNERS *Burton Hobson & Fred Reinfeld*	5.00
____	ENTERTAINING WITH ESP *Tony 'Doc' Shiels*	2.00
____	400 FASCINATING MAGIC TRICKS YOU CAN DO *Howard Thurston*	4.00
____	HOW I TURN JUNK INTO FUN AND PROFIT *Sari*	3.00
____	HOW TO WRITE A HIT SONG & SELL IT *Tommy Boyce*	7.00
____	JUGGLING MADE EASY *Rudolf Dittrich*	3.00
____	MAGIC FOR ALL AGES *Walter Gibson*	4.00
____	MAGIC MADE EASY *Byron Wels*	2.00
____	STAMP COLLECTING FOR BEGINNERS *Burton Hobson*	3.00

HORSE PLAYERS' WINNING GUIDES

____	BETTING HORSES TO WIN *Les Conklin*	5.00
____	ELIMINATE THE LOSERS *Bob McKnight*	3.00
____	HOW TO PICK WINNING HORSES *Bob McKnight*	5.00
____	HOW TO WIN AT THE RACES *Sam (The Genius) Lewin*	5.00
____	HOW YOU CAN BEAT THE RACES *Jack Kavanagh*	5.00
____	MAKING MONEY AT THE RACES *David Barr*	5.00

____ PAYDAY AT THE RACES *Les Conklin* 5.00
____ SMART HANDICAPPING MADE EASY *William Bauman* 5.00
____ SUCCESS AT THE HARNESS RACES *Barry Meadow* 5.00
____ WINNING AT THE HARNESS RACES—An Expert's Guide *Nick Cammarano* 5.00

HUMOR

____ HOW TO FLATTEN YOUR TUSH *Coach Marge Reardon* 2.00
____ HOW TO MAKE LOVE TO YOURSELF *Ron Stevens & Joy Grdnic* 3.00
____ JOKE TELLER'S HANDBOOK *Bob Orben* 5.00
____ JOKES FOR ALL OCCASIONS *Al Schock* 5.00
____ 2000 NEW LAUGHS FOR SPEAKERS *Bob Orben* 5.00
____ 2,500 JOKES TO START 'EM LAUGHING *Bob Orben* 5.00

HYPNOTISM

____ ADVANCED TECHNIQUES OF HYPNOSIS *Melvin Powers* 3.00
____ BRAINWASHING AND THE CULTS *Paul A. Verdier, Ph.D.* 3.00
____ CHILDBIRTH WITH HYPNOSIS *William S. Kroger, M.D.* 5.00
____ HOW TO SOLVE Your Sex Problems with Self-Hypnosis *Frank S. Caprio, M.D.* 5.00
____ HOW TO STOP SMOKING THRU SELF-HYPNOSIS *Leslie M. LeCron* 3.00
____ HOW TO USE AUTO-SUGGESTION EFFECTIVELY *John Duckworth* 3.00
____ HOW YOU CAN BOWL BETTER USING SELF-HYPNOSIS *Jack Heise* 4.00
____ HOW YOU CAN PLAY BETTER GOLF USING SELF-HYPNOSIS *Jack Heise* 3.00
____ HYPNOSIS AND SELF-HYPNOSIS *Bernard Hollander, M.D.* 5.00
____ HYPNOTISM *(Originally published in 1893) Carl Sextus* 5.00
____ HYPNOTISM & PSYCHIC PHENOMENA *Simeon Edmunds* 4.00
____ HYPNOTISM MADE EASY *Dr. Ralph Winn* 3.00
____ HYPNOTISM MADE PRACTICAL *Louis Orton* 5.00
____ HYPNOTISM REVEALED *Melvin Powers* 3.00
____ HYPNOTISM TODAY *Leslie LeCron and Jean Bordeaux, Ph.D.* 5.00
____ MODERN HYPNOSIS *Lesley Kuhn & Salvatore Russo, Ph.D.* 5.00
____ NEW CONCEPTS OF HYPNOSIS *Bernard C. Gindes, M.D.* 7.00
____ NEW SELF-HYPNOSIS *Paul Adams* 5.00
____ POST-HYPNOTIC INSTRUCTIONS—Suggestions for Therapy *Arnold Furst* 5.00
____ PRACTICAL GUIDE TO SELF-HYPNOSIS *Melvin Powers* 3.00
____ PRACTICAL HYPNOTISM *Philip Magonet, M.D.* 3.00
____ SECRETS OF HYPNOTISM *S. J. Van Pelt, M.D.* 5.00
____ SELF-HYPNOSIS A Conditioned-Response Technique *Laurence Sparks* 7.00
____ SELF-HYPNOSIS Its Theory, Technique & Application *Melvin Powers* 3.00
____ THERAPY THROUGH HYPNOSIS *edited by Raphael H. Rhodes* 5.00

JUDAICA

____ MODERN ISRAEL *Lily Edelman* 2.00
____ SERVICE OF THE HEART *Evelyn Garfiel, Ph.D.* 7.00
____ STORY OF ISRAEL IN COINS *Jean & Maurice Gould* 2.00
____ STORY OF ISRAEL IN STAMPS *Maxim & Gabriel Shamir* 1.00
____ TONGUE OF THE PROPHETS *Robert St. John* 7.00

JUST FOR WOMEN

____ COSMOPOLITAN'S GUIDE TO MARVELOUS MEN Fwd. by *Helen Gurley Brown* 3.00
____ COSMOPOLITAN'S HANG-UP HANDBOOK Foreword by *Helen Gurley Brown* 4.00
____ COSMOPOLITAN'S LOVE BOOK—A Guide to Ecstasy in Bed 5.00
____ COSMOPOLITAN'S NEW ETIQUETTE GUIDE Fwd. by *Helen Gurley Brown* 4.00
____ I AM A COMPLEAT WOMAN *Doris Hagopian & Karen O'Connor Sweeney* 3.00
____ JUST FOR WOMEN—A Guide to the Female Body *Richard E. Sand, M.D.* 5.00
____ NEW APPROACHES TO SEX IN MARRIAGE *John E. Eichenlaub, M.D.* 3.00
____ SEXUALLY ADEQUATE FEMALE *Frank S. Caprio, M.D.* 3.00
____ SEXUALLY FULFILLED WOMAN *Dr. Rachel Copelan* 5.00
____ YOUR FIRST YEAR OF MARRIAGE *Dr. Tom McGinnis* 3.00

MARRIAGE, SEX & PARENTHOOD

____ ABILITY TO LOVE *Dr. Allan Fromme* 6.00
____ GUIDE TO SUCCESSFUL MARRIAGE *Drs. Albert Ellis & Robert Harper* 5.00
____ HOW TO RAISE AN EMOTIONALLY HEALTHY, HAPPY CHILD *A. Ellis* 5.00
____ SEX WITHOUT GUILT *Albert Ellis, Ph.D.* 5.00
____ SEXUALLY ADEQUATE MALE *Frank S. Caprio, M.D.* 3.00

____ SEXUALLY FULFILLED MAN *Dr. Rachel Copelan* 5.00
____ STAYING IN LOVE *Dr. Norton F. Kristy* 7.00

MELVIN POWERS' MAIL ORDER LIBRARY

____ HOW TO GET RICH IN MAIL ORDER *Melvin Powers* 15.00
____ HOW TO WRITE A GOOD ADVERTISEMENT *Victor O. Schwab* 20.00
____ MAIL ORDER MADE EASY *J. Frank Brumbaugh* 20.00
____ U.S. MAIL ORDER SHOPPER'S GUIDE *Susan Spitzer* 10.00

METAPHYSICS & OCCULT

____ BOOK OF TALISMANS, AMULETS & ZODIACAL GEMS *William Pavitt* 7.00
____ CONCENTRATION—A Guide to Mental Mastery *Mouni Sadhu* 5.00
____ CRITIQUES OF GOD *Edited by Peter Angeles* 7.00
____ EXTRA-TERRESTRIAL INTELLIGENCE—The First Encounter 6.00
____ FORTUNE TELLING WITH CARDS *P. Foli* 5.00
____ HANDWRITING TELLS *Nadya Olyanova* 7.00
____ HOW TO INTERPRET DREAMS, OMENS & FORTUNE TELLING SIGNS *Gettings* 5.00
____ HOW TO UNDERSTAND YOUR DREAMS *Geoffrey A. Dudley* 3.00
____ ILLUSTRATED YOGA *William Zorn* 3.00
____ IN DAYS OF GREAT PEACE *Mouni Sadhu* 3.00
____ LSD—THE AGE OF MIND *Bernard Roseman* 2.00
____ MAGICIAN—His Training and Work *W. E. Butler* 3.00
____ MEDITATION *Mouni Sadhu* 7.00
____ MODERN NUMEROLOGY *Morris C. Goodman* 5.00
____ NUMEROLOGY—ITS FACTS AND SECRETS *Ariel Yvon Taylor* 3.00
____ NUMEROLOGY MADE EASY *W. Mykian* 5.00
____ PALMISTRY MADE EASY *Fred Gettings* 5.00
____ PALMISTRY MADE PRACTICAL *Elizabeth Daniels Squire* 5.00
____ PALMISTRY SECRETS REVEALED *Henry Frith* 4.00
____ PROPHECY IN OUR TIME *Martin Ebon* 2.50
____ SUPERSTITION—Are You Superstitious? *Eric Maple* 2.00
____ TAROT *Mouni Sadhu* 8.00
____ TAROT OF THE BOHEMIANS *Papus* 7.00
____ WAYS TO SELF-REALIZATION *Mouni Sadhu* 3.00
____ WITCHCRAFT, MAGIC & OCCULTISM—A Fascinating History *W. B. Crow* 5.00
____ WITCHCRAFT—THE SIXTH SENSE *Justine Glass* 7.00
____ WORLD OF PSYCHIC RESEARCH *Hereward Carrington* 2.00

SELF-HELP & INSPIRATIONAL

____ CHARISMA How You Can Have That "Special Magic" *Marcia Grad* 7.00
____ DAILY POWER FOR JOYFUL LIVING *Dr. Donald Curtis* 5.00
____ DYNAMIC THINKING *Melvin Powers* 5.00
____ GREATEST POWER IN THE UNIVERSE *U. S. Andersen* 5.00
____ GROW RICH WHILE YOU SLEEP *Ben Sweetland* 7.00
____ GROWTH THROUGH REASON *Albert Ellis, Ph.D.* 7.00
____ GUIDE TO PERSONAL HAPPINESS *Albert Ellis, Ph.D. & Irving Becker, Ed. D.* 5.00
____ HANDWRITING ANALYSIS MADE EASY *John Marley* 5.00
____ HELPING YOURSELF WITH APPLIED PSYCHOLOGY *R. Henderson* 2.00
____ HOW TO ATTRACT GOOD LUCK *A. H. Z. Carr* 5.00
____ HOW TO BE GREAT *Dr. Donald Curtis* 5.00
____ HOW TO DEVELOP A WINNING PERSONALITY *Martin Panzer* 5.00
____ HOW TO DEVELOP AN EXCEPTIONAL MEMORY *Young & Gibson* 5.00
____ HOW TO LIVE WITH A NEUROTIC *Albert Ellis, Ph. D.* 5.00
____ HOW TO OVERCOME YOUR FEARS *M. P. Leahy, M.D.* 3.00
____ HOW TO SUCCEED *Brian Adams* 7.00
____ HUMAN PROBLEMS & HOW TO SOLVE THEM *Dr. Donald Curtis* 5.00
____ I CAN *Ben Sweetland* 7.00
____ I WILL *Ben Sweetland* 3.00
____ LEFT-HANDED PEOPLE *Michael Barsley* 5.00
____ MAGIC IN YOUR MIND *U. S. Andersen* 7.00
____ MAGIC OF THINKING BIG *Dr. David J. Schwartz* 3.00
____ MAGIC POWER OF YOUR MIND *Walter M. Germain* 7.00
____ MENTAL POWER THROUGH SLEEP SUGGESTION *Melvin Powers* 3.00

_____ NEVER UNDERESTIMATE THE SELLING POWER OF A WOMAN *Dottie Walters* 7.00
_____ NEW GUIDE TO RATIONAL LIVING *Albert Ellis, Ph.D. & R. Harper, Ph.D.* 3.00
_____ PROJECT YOU *A Manual of Rational Assertiveness Training Paris & Casey* 6.00
_____ PSYCHO-CYBERNETICS *Maxwell Maltz, M.D.* 5.00
_____ PSYCHOLOGY OF HANDWRITING *Nadya Olyanova* 7.00
_____ SALES CYBERNETICS *Brian Adams* 7.00
_____ SCIENCE OF MIND IN DAILY LIVING *Dr. Donald Curtis* 5.00
_____ SECRET OF SECRETS *U. S. Andersen* 7.00
_____ SECRET POWER OF THE PYRAMIDS *U. S. Andersen* 7.00
_____ SELF-THERAPY FOR THE STUTTERER *Malcolm Frazer* 3.00
_____ STUTTERING AND WHAT YOU CAN DO ABOUT IT *W. Johnson, Ph.D.* 2.50
_____ SUCCESS-CYBERNETICS *U. S. Andersen* 6.00
_____ 10 DAYS TO A GREAT NEW LIFE *William E. Edwards* 3.00
_____ THINK AND GROW RICH *Napoleon Hill* 5.00
_____ THINK YOUR WAY TO SUCCESS *Dr. Lew Losoncy* 5.00
_____ THREE MAGIC WORDS *U. S. Andersen* 7.00
_____ TREASURY OF COMFORT *edited by Rabbi Sidney Greenberg* 5.00
_____ TREASURY OF THE ART OF LIVING *Sidney S. Greenberg* 5.00
_____ WHAT YOUR HANDWRITING REVEALS *Albert E. Hughes* 3.00
_____ YOU ARE NOT THE TARGET *Laura Huxley* 5.00
_____ YOUR SUBCONSCIOUS POWER *Charles M. Simmons* 5.00
_____ YOUR THOUGHTS CAN CHANGE YOUR LIFE *Dr. Donald Curtis* 5.00

SPORTS

_____ BICYCLING FOR FUN AND GOOD HEALTH *Kenneth E. Luther* 2.00
_____ BILLIARDS—Pocket • Carom • Three Cushion *Clive Cottingham, Jr.* 5.00
_____ CAMPING-OUT 101 Ideas & Activities *Bruno Knobel* 2.00
_____ COMPLETE GUIDE TO FISHING *Vlad Evanoff* 2.00
_____ HOW TO IMPROVE YOUR RACQUETBALL *Lubarsky Kaufman & Scagnetti* 3.00
_____ HOW TO WIN AT POCKET BILLIARDS *Edward D. Knuchell* 5.00
_____ JOY OF WALKING *Jack Scagnetti* 3.00
_____ LEARNING & TEACHING SOCCER SKILLS *Eric Worthington* 3.00
_____ MOTORCYCLING FOR BEGINNERS *I. G. Edmonds* 3.00
_____ RACQUETBALL FOR WOMEN *Toni Hudson, Jack Scagnetti & Vince Rondone* 3.00
_____ RACQUETBALL MADE EASY *Steve Lubarsky, Rod Delson & Jack Scagnetti* 5.00
_____ SECRET OF BOWLING STRIKES *Dawson Taylor* 5.00
_____ SECRET OF PERFECT PUTTING *Horton Smith & Dawson Taylor* 5.00
_____ SOCCER—The Game & How to Play It *Gary Rosenthal* 5.00
_____ STARTING SOCCER *Edward F. Dolan, Jr.* 3.00

TENNIS LOVERS' LIBRARY

_____ BEGINNER'S GUIDE TO WINNING TENNIS *Helen Hull Jacobs* 2.00
_____ HOW TO BEAT BETTER TENNIS PLAYERS *Loring Fiske* 4.00
_____ HOW TO IMPROVE YOUR TENNIS—Style, Strategy & Analysis *C. Wilson* 2.00
_____ PLAY TENNIS WITH ROSEWALL *Ken Rosewall* 2.00
_____ PSYCH YOURSELF TO BETTER TENNIS *Dr. Walter A. Luszki* 2.00
_____ TENNIS FOR BEGINNERS, *Dr. H. A. Murray* 2.00
_____ TENNIS MADE EASY *Joel Brecheen* 4.00
_____ WEEKEND TENNIS—How to Have Fun & Win at the Same Time *Bill Talbert* 3.00
_____ WINNING WITH PERCENTAGE TENNIS—Smart Strategy *Jack Lowe* 2.00

WILSHIRE PET LIBRARY

_____ DOG OBEDIENCE TRAINING *Gust Kessopulos* 5.00
_____ DOG TRAINING MADE EASY & FUN *John W. Kellogg* 4.00
_____ HOW TO BRING UP YOUR PET DOG *Kurt Unkelbach* 2.00
_____ HOW TO RAISE & TRAIN YOUR PUPPY *Jeff Griffen* 5.00
_____ PIGEONS: HOW TO RAISE & TRAIN THEM *William H. Allen, Jr.* 2.00

The books listed above can be obtained from your book dealer or directly from Melvin Powers. When ordering, please remit $1.00 postage for the first book and 50¢ for each additional book.

Melvin Powers

12015 Sherman Road, No. Hollywood, California 91605

WILSHIRE HORSE LOVERS' LIBRARY

	Title	Price
____	AMATEUR HORSE BREEDER *A. C. Leighton Hardman*	5.00
____	AMERICAN QUARTER HORSE IN PICTURES *Margaret Cabell Self*	3.00
____	APPALOOSA HORSE *Donna & Bill Richardson*	7.00
____	ARABIAN HORSE *Reginald S. Summerhays*	5.00
____	ART OF WESTERN RIDING *Suzanne Norton Jones*	5.00
____	AT THE HORSE SHOW *Margaret Cabell Self*	3.00
____	BACK-YARD HORSE *Peggy Jett Pittinger*	4.00
____	BASIC DRESSAGE *Jean Froissard*	5.00
____	BEGINNER'S GUIDE TO HORSEBACK RIDING *Sheila Wall*	2.00
____	BEGINNER'S GUIDE TO THE WESTERN HORSE *Natlee Kenoyer*	2.00
____	BITS—THEIR HISTORY, USE AND MISUSE *Louis Taylor*	5.00
____	BREAKING & TRAINING THE DRIVING HORSE *Doris Ganton*	10.00
____	BREAKING YOUR HORSE'S BAD HABITS *W. Dayton Sumner*	7.00
____	COMPLETE TRAINING OF HORSE AND RIDER *Colonel Alois Podhajsky*	6.00
____	DISORDERS OF THE HORSE & WHAT TO DO ABOUT THEM *E. Hanauer*	5.00
____	DOG TRAINING MADE EASY & FUN *John W. Kellogg*	4.00
____	DRESSAGE—A Study of the Finer Points in Riding *Henry Wynmalen*	7.00
____	DRIVE ON *Doris Ganton*	7.00
____	DRIVING HORSES *Sallie Walrond*	5.00
____	EQUITATION *Jean Froissard*	5.00
____	FIRST AID FOR HORSES *Dr. Charles H. Denning, Jr.*	5.00
____	FUN OF RAISING A COLT *Rubye & Frank Griffith*	5.00
____	FUN ON HORSEBACK *Margaret Caball Self*	4.00
____	GYMKHANA GAMES *Natlee Kenoyer*	2.00
____	HORSE DISEASES—Causes, Symptoms & Treatment *Dr. H. G. Belschner*	7.00
____	HORSE OWNER'S CONCISE GUIDE *Elsie V. Hanauer*	3.00
____	HORSE SELECTION & CARE FOR BEGINNERS *George H. Conn*	7.00
____	HORSEBACK RIDING FOR BEGINNERS *Louis Taylor*	7.00
____	HORSEBACK RIDING MADE EASY & FUN *Sue Henderson Coen*	7.00
____	HORSES—Their Selection, Care & Handling *Margaret Cabell Self*	5.00
____	HOW TO BUY A BETTER HORSE & SELL THE HORSE YOU OWN	3.00
____	HOW TO ENJOY YOUR QUARTER HORSE *Willard H. Porter*	3.00
____	HUNTER IN PICTURES *Margaret Cabell Self*	2.00
____	ILLUSTRATED BOOK OF THE HORSE *S. Sidney* (8½" × 11")	10.00
____	ILLUSTRATED HORSE MANAGEMENT—400 Illustrations *Dr. E. Mayhew*	6.00
____	ILLUSTRATED HORSE TRAINING *Captain M. H. Hayes*	7.00
____	ILLUSTRATED HORSEBACK RIDING FOR BEGINNERS *Jeanne Mellin*	3.00
____	JUMPING—Learning & Teaching *Jean Froissard*	5.00
____	KNOW ALL ABOUT HORSES *Harry Disston*	3.00
____	LAME HORSE Cause, Symptoms & Treatment *Dr. James R. Rooney*	7.00
____	LAW & YOUR HORSE *Edward H. Greene*	7.00
____	MANUAL OF HORSEMANSHIP *Harold Black*	5.00
____	MOVIE HORSES—The Fascinating Techniques of Training *Anthony Amaral*	2.00
____	POLICE HORSES *Judith Campbell*	2.00
____	PRACTICAL GUIDE TO HORSESHOEING	5.00
____	PRACTICAL GUIDE TO OWNING YOUR OWN HORSE *Steven D. Price*	3.00
____	PRACTICAL HORSE PSYCHOLOGY *Moyra Williams*	5.00
____	PROBLEM HORSES Guide for Curing Serious Behavior Habits *Summerhays*	4.00
____	REINSMAN OF THE WEST—BRIDLES & BITS *Ed Connell*	5.00
____	RIDE WESTERN *Louis Taylor*	5.00
____	SCHOOLING YOUR YOUNG HORSE *George Wheatley*	5.00
____	STABLE MANAGEMENT FOR THE OWNER-GROOM *George Wheatley*	4.00
____	STALLION MANAGEMENT—A Guide for Stud Owners *A. C. Hardman*	5.00
____	TEACHING YOUR HORSE TO JUMP *W. J. Froud*	5.00
____	TRAINING YOUR HORSE TO SHOW *Neale Haley*	5.00
____	TREATING COMMON DISEASES OF YOUR HORSE *Dr. George H. Conn*	5.00
____	YOU AND YOUR PONY *Pepper Mainwaring Healey* (8½" × 11")	6.00
____	YOUR FIRST HORSE *George C. Saunders, M.D.*	5.00
____	YOUR PONY BOOK *Hermann Wiederhold*	2.00

The books listed above can be obtained from your book dealer or directly from Melvin Powers. When ordering, please remit $1.00 postage for the first book and 50¢ for each additional book.

Melvin Powers

12015 Sherman Road, No. Hollywood, California 91605

Melvin Powers' Favorite Books

HOW TO GET RICH IN MAIL ORDER

by Melvin Powers

Contents:
1. How to Develop Your Mail Order Expertise 2. How to Find a Unique Product or Service to Sell 3. How to Make Money with Classified Ads 4. How to Make Money with Display Ads 5. The Unlimited Potential for Making Money with Direct Mail 6. How to Copycat Successful Mail Order Operations 7. How I Created A Best Seller Using the Copycat Technique 8. How to Start and Run a Profitable Mail Order, Special Interest Book or Record Business 9. I Enjoy Selling Books by Mail—Some of My Successful and Not-So-Successful Ads and Direct Mail Circulars 10. Five of My Most Successful Direct Mail Pieces That Sold and Are Still Selling Millions of Dollars Worth of Books 11. Melvin Powers' Mail Order Success Strategy—Follow It and You'll Become a Millionaire 12. How to Sell Your Products to Mail Order Companies, Retail Outlets, Jobbers, and Fund Raisers for Maximum Distribution and Profits 13. How to Get Free Display Ads and Publicity That Can Put You on the Road to Riches 14. How to Make Your Advertising Copy Sizzle to Make You Wealthy 15. Questions and Answers to Help You Get Started Making Money in Your Own Mail Order Business 16. A Personal Word from Melvin Powers **8½" x 11" — 352 Pages . . . $16 postpaid**

HOW TO SELF-PUBLISH YOUR BOOK AND HAVE THE FUN AND EXCITEMENT OF BEING A BEST-SELLING AUTHOR

by Melvin Powers

An expert's step-by-step guide to marketing your book successfully

176 Pages . . . $11.00 postpaid

A NEW GUIDE TO RATIONAL LIVING

by Albert Ellis, Ph.D. & Robert A. Harper, Ph.D.

Contents:
1. How Far Can You Go With Self-Analysis? 2. You Feel the Way You Think 3. Feeling Well by Thinking Straight 4. How You Create Your Feelings 5. Thinking Yourself Out of Emotional Disturbances 6. Recognizing and Attacking Neurotic Behavior 7. Overcoming the Influences of the Past 8. Does Reason Always Prove Reasonable? 9. Refusing to Feel Desperately Unhappy 10. Tackling Dire Needs for Approval 11. Eradicating Dire Fears of Failure 12. How to Stop Blaming and Start Living 13. How to Feel Undepressed though Frustrated 14. Controlling Your Own Destiny 15. Conquering Anxiety

256 Pages . . . $3.50 postpaid

PSYCHO-CYBERNETICS

A New Technique for Using Your Subconscious Power

by Maxwell Maltz, M.D., F.I.C.S.

Contents:
1. The Self Image: Your Key to a Better Life 2. Discovering the Success Mechanism Within You 3. Imagination—The First Key to Your Success Mechanism 4. Dehypnotize Yourself from False Beliefs 5. How to Utilize the Power of Rational Thinking 6. Relax and Let Your Success Mechanism Work for You 7. You Can Acquire the Habit of Happiness 8. Ingredients of the Success-Type Personality and How to Acquire Them 9. The Failure Mechanism: How to Make It Work For You Instead of Against You 10. How to Remove Emotional Scars, or How to Give Yourself an Emotional Face Lift 11. How to Unlock Your Real Personality 12. Do-It-Yourself Tranquilizers **288 Pages . . . $5.50 postpaid**

A PRACTICAL GUIDE TO SELF-HYPNOSIS

by Melvin Powers

Contents:
1. What You Should Know About Self-Hypnosis 2. What About the Dangers of Hypnosis? 3. Is Hypnosis the Answer? 4. How Does Self-Hypnosis Work? 5. How to Arouse Yourself from the Self-Hypnotic State 6. How to Attain Self-Hypnosis 7. Deepening the Self-Hypnotic State 8. What You Should Know About Becoming an Excellent Subject 9. Techniques for Reaching the Somnambulistic State 10. A New Approach to Self-Hypnosis When All Else Fails 11. Psychological Aids and Their Function 12. The Nature of Hypnosis 13. Practical Applications of Self-Hypnosis **128 Pages . . . $3.50 postpaid**

The books listed above can be obtained from your book dealer or directly from Melvin Powers. When ordering, please remit $1.00 postage for the first book and 50¢ for each additional book.

Melvin Powers

12015 Sherman Road, No. Hollywood, California 91605

Notes

Notes

Notes

Notes

Notes